Jane's

B ook

Group

ISBN 0710620012

Published by
Jane's Information Group
1340 Braddock Place, Suite 300 Alexandria, VA 22314 USA
Sentinel House, 163 Brighton Road, Coulsdon, Surrey
CR5 2YH UK

First printing August 1999

Contents

Introduction

The conflict in the Balkans has become a recognition nightmare. Within the borders of the former Yugoslavia there are now five countries, two federal republics, three further ethnic regions and over 40 foreign powers keeping the peace. This book is designed as an aid to recognition, listing principal equipment, camouflage patterns and insignia used by former Yugoslav, NATO and Coalition forces.

Included in this book are the combat aircraft, transport aircraft, helicopters, tanks, reconnaissance vehicles, armoured personnel carriers, self-propelled and towed artillery systems, in widespread use by all sides. Anti-aircraft artillery, surface-to-air missiles, small arms and mortars used by former Yugoslav forces are also included. The list of weapons covers small arms in use with major military and police forces only. One can expect to see many more exotic weapons in use with paramilitaries and ethnic guerrilla forces.

There are four recognition sections. The colour pages show uniform, insignia and where possible rank structure of major armies and contributors to peacekeeping operations. The black section covers equipment used by former Yugoslav forces and the white section details NATO/Coalition equipment. To avoid confusion a grey section between them covers equipment in use by both sides.

Terrain and Climate

Located in the geographic centre of the Balkans, the Federal Republic of Yugoslavia comprises two republics Serbia and Montenegro, and two provinces, Vojvodina and Kosovo.

Kosovo is the smallest of the four regions and lies in the very south of the country. Roughly the same size as Northern Ireland, Kosovo resembles a huge bowl. A large open plain dominates the centre of the province, lying at an altitude of 750 m above sea level. Surrounding the plain on all sides are a series of high mountain ranges, with peaks reaching 2,000 m. On the plain most land is turned over to farming, with few major towns and many villages. Metalled roads link the major urban areas within the central plain, where off-road movement is feasible. Montenegro and Serbia line the northern and eastern borders, while Albania and the Former Yugoslav Republic of Macedonia (FYROM) line the western and southern borders.

Montenegro is the second smallest Yugoslav region, and is unique in retaining its own parliament, which sits in Podgorica. Montenegro also boasts Yugoslavia's sole coastline, via a narrow low-lying coastal strip along the Adriatic. Beyond this the interior terrain is a maze of steep valleys and high mountains making any movement off-road impossible to either wheeled or tracked vehicles. Most of Montenegro lies above 1,500 m and is heavily forested. The only open land runs from the capital towards the Albanian border in the extreme south, around the large lake of Skadarsko Jez.

Vojvodina is a large flat region that lies in the extreme north of Yugoslavia, along the border with Hungary. It is bisected by a number of rivers not least the very wide Danube and Sava. The open well-watered plains make it the most fertile region, with many large-scale farms. Most major bridges have been destroyed by NATO airstrikes, making large scale movement very difficult.

Serbia is the largest and most heavily populated region of Yugoslavia. In the north where it meets Vojvodina it is flat and open. As you travel south the ground becomes progressively steeper and more mountainous. The capital Belgrade sits on the Danube where it changes direction and cuts Serbia in two. One major motorway runs north/south from FYROM to Nis and then Belgrade, providing good communications. Other major urban areas are linked by all-weather metalled roads. However many of the rural roads are single track and prone to closure during severe weather. Many bridges have been destroyed and mass movement can be described as difficult.

FYROM split from Yugoslavia in 1992 and is now a separate country. Landlocked, heavily forested and prone to sudden earthquakes, most of the country lies above 900 m. The only flat land lies in the east, where a wide valley acts as a natural corridor from north to south. The main Salonika-Belgrade motorway runs through this region providing the country's main supply route.

Most of the population lives in this eastern area. Roads and communications along the mountainous Albanian and Bulgarian borders is strictly limited. The land is poorly drained and flooding is common.

Albania borders FYROM and Kosovo to the east and Montenegro to the north. Three quarters of the country is above 2,000 m and heavily forested. Most of the population lives in the broad coastal plain that runs north to south along the Adriatic coast. Albania is a very rural country where car ownership has only been allowed since 1991. Consequently, the further you get from the coastal plain, roads disappear and those that remain are prone to subsidence and erosion. The country is subject to severe earthquakes. Over 100,000 people were killed by a huge earthquake in 1979.

Despite the huge differences in terrain the climate throughout the region is fairly similar. A moderate continental climate prevails in low-lying areas. Winters are harsh in the mountainous regions, which suffer from early falls of snow which can last well into spring. A northern wind, the Kosava, brings cold air from the Carpathian mountains which can lower the average winter temperatures to -2°C.

Average temperature in the summer is a dry 22°C. The influences of the Mediterranean climate along the coast create some of the highest rainfall levels in Europe, over 5,000 mm in some areas.

Historical Overview

Origins

Kosovo holds a very important place in Serbian history and culture. Medieval Serbia was a powerful state, which held sway over much of the Balkans from the 12th to 14th century. In 1217 Serbia conquered Kosovo and the land was handed over to the Serb Orthodox Church. Even today the majority of Serb Orthodox religious sites and monasteries remain in Kosovo. This period is regarded as the golden age of Serbian culture and influence.

This golden age ended with the Ottoman Turk invasion in the early 1300s. By the end of the century, Serbia was fighting to maintain control of its borders. In June 1389, a coalition of Serbs, Bulgars, Bosnians and Albanians met the Ottoman army outside Pristina in the Battle of Kosovo Polje, the "Field of Blackbirds". Over 60,000 men took part in the battle in which both the Serb leader Prince Lazar and the Ottoman Emir were killed.

The events of 1389 remain a permanent focal point of Serbian national identity. Prince Lazar assumed legendary status as a heroic Serbian leader. Nevertheless, Serbia paid a heavy price for the losses suffered at the Field of Blackbirds. Within 50 years the Turks had occupied most of Serbia, Albania, Bulgaria and Bosnia. Only Montenegro held out against the invaders, a point of some pride among Montenegrins. For over four centuries the Ottoman Turks ruled the southern half of the Balkans, outlawing Christianity and converting many of the Balkan people to Islam. Serbia was destroyed as an independent nation and many of its people were forced to flee north.

The declining powers of the Ottoman Empire encouraged the suppressed Balkan nations to seek independence. Turkey recognised Serbian independence and ceded substantial territory under the 1878 Treaty of San Stefano. Independence was reaffirmed under the Treaty of Berlin but territorial cuts caused much bitterness among the Serbs as the Austro-Hungarian Empire annexed Bosnia-Herzegovina. Disputes over these lands led to increasing tension between Serbia and Austro-Hungary.

In Sarajevo in 1914, a Serb nationalist assassinated Archduke Ferdinand, heir to the Austro-Hungarian throne. Austro-Hungary responded by invading Serbia, triggering the chain of events which led to the outbreak of the First World War. The war went badly for Serbia and the entire country was occupied by Austro-Hungary. Serb forces, joined by Greek, French and British troops, began to retake land during the 1917-18 campaign but the cost had been high. Over a million Serbs and Montenegrins were killed, from a population of less than 10 million.

The Creation of Yugoslavia

For its part in the war effort, Serbia was given Bosnia from Austro-Hungary. A Kingdom of Serbs, Croats and

Slovenes was formed in 1919. This new state was renamed the Kingdom of Yugoslavia in 1929. Serbia was the main power within the new state and the first inklings of civil war were stirred in 1934 when the King of Yugoslavia, a Serb, was killed by a Croat nationalist.

In 1941 Germany invaded Yugoslavia to assist Italy's flagging war in Greece. Yugoslavia fell under German and Italian occupation but numerous partisan groups sprang up to combat the invaders. The volatile relationship between Croatia and Serbia was exploited by Axis forces who set individual partisan groups against each other.

Around this time Josip Broz Tito, a Croat, emerged as the leader of the largest partisan group, the communists. He arranged a series of shaky alliances between royalist, communist, Serb, Croat, Albanian, Montenegrin and Macedonian partisans. With weapons and assistance from the UK and US he launched a series of bloody guerrilla offensives against Germany and its Croat nationalist puppet government.

Yet again the cost in human lives was extreme. Five million Yugoslavs died in concentration camps, through starvation, mass executions and the constant fighting. Nevertheless, by 1945 Yugoslavia had become the only country in Europe to liberate itself without the intervention of US, UK or Russian ground troops.

Tito established a communist government at the end of the war. His primary aim was to stamp out any remaining ethnic nationalism which could lead to conflict within Yugoslavia. A federalist system was used to accommodate the various ethnic minorities. All of the republics were allocated extensive powers. Kosovo and Vojvodina were also given a considerable degree of self-government. This federal system and Tito's influence maintained peace in Yugoslavia for 50 years. When Tito died in 1980 nationalist leaders began to undermine his achievements.

The Demise of Yugoslavia

By the late 1980s Slovenia and Croatia were calling for independence from Yugoslavia. The possible break up of Yugoslavia concerned Serb nationalists, who saw it as a threat to their dominant position. In 1987 Slobodan Milosevic became Leader of the League of Communists. He used his position to exploit nationalist fever in Serbia and assume greater control of the country. In 1989 he abolished the autonomous governments in Kosovo and Vojvodina and began calling for a greater Serbia, which would unify all Serb areas under one government.

In 1991 Croatia and Slovenia announced their intention to break away from Yugoslavia. With the support of Milosevic, the Serb dominated People's Yugoslav Army (JNA) moved in to isolate Slovenia, seizing all border crossing points and the airport. They suffered a humiliating defeat at the hands of well-prepared Slovenian militia forces using guerrilla tactics. The JNA was forced to depart from Slovenia, leaving all its heavy equipment behind.

The focus of events fell on Croatia. JNA troops retreating from Slovenia found themselves under attack by disorganized Croat mobs. The Serb presidency used those JNA forces and Serb nationalist paramilitaries to take and hold as much land as possible. Civil war erupted, degenerating into a military stalemate and large scale evictions and massacres by both sides. A ceasefire in 1992 left the Serbian minority in control of 30 per cent of Croatia. This area was established as the Krajina autonomous region and later became a cause of renewed conflict between Croatia and Serbia. In 1995 Croatian army units mounted a massive offensive against the Krajina expelling hundreds of thousands of Serbs. Many of those Serb refugees found their way to Belgrade, Bosnia and in large numbers Kosovo.

In April 1992 fighting broke out in Bosnia. Divided three ways ethnically, Bosnia broke apart into Croatian, Serb and Muslim enclaves. The Bosnian Serbs were supported directly by JNA units and managed to seize most of the dominating ground. Serbia and Montenegro announced a new Federal Republic of Yugoslavia. The JNA was renamed the Yugoslav Army (VJ). Macedonia was given its independence but Kosovo and Vojvodina remained under the direct control of Belgrade.

The war in Bosnia dragged on until 1995, sucking in more and more peacekeeping resources from the UN and eventually NATO. A military alliance between the Croat and Muslim Bosnians turned the advantage against the Bosnian Serbs who suffered a series of defeats. The VJ did not intervene when NATO launched air strikes against the Bosnian Serbs and Milosevic himself played an important part in getting NATO/UN hostages released. Belgrade was distancing itself from the Bosnian Serbs in an attempt to have the crippling embargoes on Yugoslavia lifted.

By late 1995, the Bosnian Serbs had yielded to pressure from Belgrade to stop the war. Milosevic signed the Dayton Peace Accord, which ended the conflict in Bosnia. Following this the international community lifted some sanctions against Yugoslavia. However, broader sanctions were maintained because of the lack of co-operation from Belgrade with the war crimes tribunals.

The Albanian Influence

The outbreak of war in the former Yugoslavia increased tension throughout Albania. With ethnic Albanians forming approximately 90 per cent of the population in the Yugoslav province of Kosovo, concern focused on a possible Serbian backlash. Belgrade's claim that Tirana provided training bases and arms shipments to Kosovan separatists in late 1992-93 were denied by the Albanian government.

The collapse of government-endorsed pyramid trading schemes in the spring of 1997 left thousands of Albanians penniless. Many individuals suspected of being involved in the pyramid fraud were linked closely with President Sali Berisha. In the rioting which ensued, tens of thousands of weapons, including heavy armour, were stolen from police headquarters and army garrisons.

Reports concluded that 2,000 people were killed and 1,500 military depots were looted.

An Italian-led military force committed under Operation 'Alba' arrived in June 1997 to ensure that security did not break down during the elections. Although the force was prevented from directly intervening in Albania's affairs, its presence succeeded in providing a measure of calm at a dangerous time.

The Kosovo Crisis

In Kosovo several Albanian separatist movements had been operating against Belgrade since the early 1980s. In 1981 an attempt to demand a fully-fledged Kosovo republic was crushed by Federal army and police units. Between 1991 and 1995, while Belgrade focused on Croatia and Bosnia, attacks on police units by Kosovar Albanian guerrillas increased. The Kosovo Liberation Army (UCK) emerged as the leading power among anti-Belgrade forces and began to threaten government control of the region.

On 22 April 1996 the UCK launched four simultaneous attacks on police stations, killing three Serb civilians, two policemen and wounding many more. Belgrade responded by calling up army reservists into the police paramilitary forces and deploying them against villages under rebel control. UCK attacks were mainly directed towards police and paramilitary forces. However, it also targeted ethnic Albanians from rival groups who refused to join the UCK.

Yugoslav police launched a series of arrest operations in January 1997 but by September the UCK had intensified its campaign with 10 co-ordinated attacks across Kosovo. Anti-tank weapons were used in later attacks and in response Belgrade began supplying police and paramilitary forces with army tank and artillery units.

In the summer of 1998 the UCK made a tactical error by trying to take and hold several villages. By trying to fight the Yugoslav forces directly, the UCK showed its weakness in numbers, tactics and equipment. Yugoslav army and police units responded quickly, grabbing major border points and launching a series of attacks against UCK villages. Reprisals against ethnic Albanian villages led to calls from the international community for a peace-keeping force to be sent in to separate the warring sides.

Escalating fighting demanded a greater call-up of Yugoslav reservists. Many reservists in Montenegro and Vojvodina refused the draft, making it a primarily Serb, not Yugoslav, force operating against the UCK. This refusal to fight in Kosovo has caused tension between Belgrade and elements of the Montenegrin population, a growing number of whom are beginning to ask for greater autonomy and even independence. In response the VJ has been involved in some barely concealed attempts to destabilise the Montenegrin government, increasing fears of a Belgrade-sanctioned coup.

In October 1998, a US brokered agreement with Belgrade promised a reduction in numbers of VJ and police units in Kosovo and the admission of international observers to monitor a ceasefire. The agreement collapsed when Yugoslav forces continued to operate against the UCK. An alleged massacre by Serb paramilitaries of 50 ethnic Albanians increased tension between Belgrade and the international community. Under the threat of air strikes Yugoslav officials agreed to peace talks with Kosovar Albanian delegations in Rambouillet, France.

After the second round of negotiations the Yugoslav delegation refused to sign any accord and walked out. Within days, reports of large-scale ethnic cleansing came out of Kosovo. In March 1999, NATO responded to the Serb actions by launching a series of airstrikes against military and civil infrastructure in Kosovo and Serbia. Belgrade responded by declaring a state of war against NATO countries and began a mass policy of ethnic cleansing. An estimated 900,000 Kosovar Albanians were forced from their homes.

After a three month bombing campaign, and with NATO forces preparing for a ground invasion, Milosevic agreed a withdrawal of his forces. NATO troops entered Kosovo without resistance, establishing a secure base for humanitarian operations and the return of the Kosovar refugees. The Serb population fearful of reprisals from the UCK, fled from Kosovo creating a new refugee problem.

Military Overview

Chain of Command

President of FRY

Supreme Defence Council

General Staff

Ground Forces | Navy | Air Force & Air Defence

Origins of the VJ

The Cold War defence doctrine of the former Yugoslavia, was designed to resist Soviet-led forces across the open plains of northern Croatia and Serbia. Two forces grew up to counter the Soviet threat, the People's Yugoslav Army (JNA) and the Territorial Defence Forces (TDF).

The JNA was a large, conventionally equipped force, designed to operate in the flatter terrain of northern Yugoslavia, acting as a mechanised first line of defence. The TDF was deployed in each of the six republics to conduct irregular partisan operations against invaders. TDF forces were raised, organised and paid by each individual republic. TDFs mirrored the ethnic majority of each republic, while the JNA was ethnically mixed. When the former Yugoslavia began to break up these TDFs provided each republic with their own, trained and equipped guerrilla force.

In June and July 1991 the Slovene TDF and the JNA fought for control of Slovenia's border checkpoints and vital positions. Slovene officers and soldiers in the JNA and officials in the ministry of defence defected on the outbreak of hostilities, helping the independence cause. The paralysis of the JNA in these first few months led to a Belgrade-sanctioned purge of all non-Serb officers and many Croat and Bosnian soldiers from the military.

When Serbia and Montenegro formed the new federal Yugoslavia in 1994, the JNA changed its name to the VJ (*Vojska Jugoslavije*). The new force had been purged of all senior generals considered disloyal or a potential threat to Milosevic. Other senior officers were purged because of their tendency to act independently. A number of high-ranking officers of the Yugoslav Air Force were forced into early retirement for suspected political links with extreme nationalists. General Panic, the chief of the General Staff, and several of his aides were also dismissed because of their links with the former prime minister, Milan Panic. These frequent dismissals and defeats in Slovenia, Croatia and Bosnia-Herzegovina thoroughly demoralised the VJ.

VJ's Internal Problems

A lack of housing forced some 11,000 officers and NCOs with 30,000 family members to live inside military barracks. Poor salaries and a lack of social prestige also contributed to a decline in morale. Some 18,000 officers and NCOs and 40,000 of their families are currently without a place to live. With the large-scale destruction of barracks by NATO air strikes this situation has got much worse. In 1994 1,750 officers and 1,240 civilians left the VJ, another 4,000 highly skilled regular members have since resigned, to find better jobs.

The Serbian Interior Ministry Police (MUP) has become Milosevic's favoured force. He rewards the loyalty of MUP personnel by providing them with better pay and higher social status than army officers. Salaries of the armed forces personnel remain low and are not regularly paid. Three-month delays have become the norm. When the MUP could no longer control Kosovo in 1998 the army gained a more prominent role. Milosevic was careful to use generals he trusted and may have bypassed the regular chain of command, issuing orders directly to General Nebojsa Pavkovic, Commander of VJ's 3rd Army. This caused anger in Montenegro where it was seen as an unconstitutional order. Following the VJ's actions in Kosovo, thousands of young Yugoslavs have refused conscription.

Ethnic minorities previously provided 50 per cent of the annual call-up but since the break-up of Yugoslavia they have been conscripted on a selective basis. Ethnic Albanians have not been called up since 1990. This is partly a reflection of the difficulty in controlling ethnically mixed units but also a conscious decision to avoid providing ethnic Albanians with basic military training. Shortages of NCOs and officers have led the VJ to significantly lower entry standards for military schools and academies.

ARMY

Chain of Command

Mechanised Corps

- 252nd (A) Armoured Brigade
- 1st (A) Mechanised Brigade
- 2nd (A) Mechanised Brigade
- 3nd (A) Mechanised Brigade
- 35th (R) Motorised Brigade
- 1st Mixed Artillery Brigade

Novi Sad Corps

- 36th (A) Mechanised Brigade
- 453rd (A) Mechanised Brigade
- 12th (A) Mechanised Brigade
- 18th (R) Motorised Brigade
- 127th (R) Light Infantry Brigade
- 16th (A) Mixed Artillery Brigade
- 16th (A) Mixed Anti-Tank

Kragujevac Corps

- 51st (A) Mechanised Brigade
- 80th (R) Motorised Brigade
- 130th (R) Motorised Brigade
- 129th (R) Light Motorised Brigade
- 20th (R) Light Infantry Brigade
- 21st (R) Light Infantry Brigade
- 24th (R) Mixed Artillery Regiment

- Special Forces Corps (Pancevo)
  - Motorised Guards Brigade (Belgrade)
  - 63rd Airborne Brigade (Nis)
  - 72nd Special Brigade

VJ ORBAT

The VJ has an active fighting strength of 90,000 troops, including 40,000 one-year conscripts. Up to 15,000 reservists were mobilised during the NATO airstrikes in 1999, and soldiers ending their conscription term are not being released.

The operational chain of command extends from the Supreme Defence Council to the Army General Staff to the numbered armies and special-purpose forces in the field. The three armies are headquartered in Belgrade, Podgorica and Nis. Army commanders report directly to the chief of the General Staff in Belgrade. The maximum strength of a corps is 15,000. A Special Forces Command was created in 1995 from the former Special Forces Corps. Establishment was the 1st (Guards) Brigade of 1,820 men in Belgrade, the 63rd (Airborne) Brigade of 605 men at Nis and the 72nd (Special) Brigade at Pancevo, with 1,074 men.

In November 1998 Chief of Staff, General Momcilo Perisic was dismissed. He later admitted it was due to his reluctance to fight NATO. The head of the Air Force General Ljubisa Velickovic also resigned in October 1998 over the deal which limited his operations over

Kosovo and allowed NATO surveillance flights. General Pavkovic the commander of the Nis-based 3rd Army, responsible for Kosovo, gained prominence after the VJ assumed an active role fighting the UCK. Pavkovic won three promotions within seven months and is considered unquestionably loyal to Milosevic, from whom he allegedly takes direct orders. Six high ranking generals in the VJ are considered potential war criminals.

Some major changes in the army's tactical doctrine have been based on combat experience gained against Croatia and Bosnia. The new doctrine still requires a mechanised brigade of 42 main battle tanks (M-84As or T-55s) to be supported in the assault by 52 armoured personnel carriers (M60s or M-80s), from which the infantry will dismount and engage on foot. Three batteries of four 122 mm D-30 field howitzers and six anti-tank guided weapon (ATGW) launchers would support flanks. The standard reserve motorised brigade within the mechanised corps does not have MBT or APC support but is equipped with 105 mm howitzers, 120 mm mortars and M10/36 or M18 self-propelled guns.

Yugoslav Air Force

The principal elements of the Yugoslav Air Force & Air Defence Command (JRV i PVO) are the Air Corps Command and the Air Defence Corps. The latter consists of surface-to-air missile (SAM) battalions and anti-aircraft artillery (AAA) regiments and the units of 'Military Information, Reporting and Vectoring (VOJIN)'.

During the NATO air campaign the majority of JRV MiG-29s and MiG-21s were destroyed; A number of J-22 and G-4 ground attack aircraft were also destroyed but many remain in service. Many transport aircraft may have also been written off. NATO air planners were impressed by the electronic discipline of the Yugoslav SAM units. Many of the primary air defence systems are still available, as they maintained electronic silence and did not engage the larger NATO formations.

AIR FORCE

Chain of Command

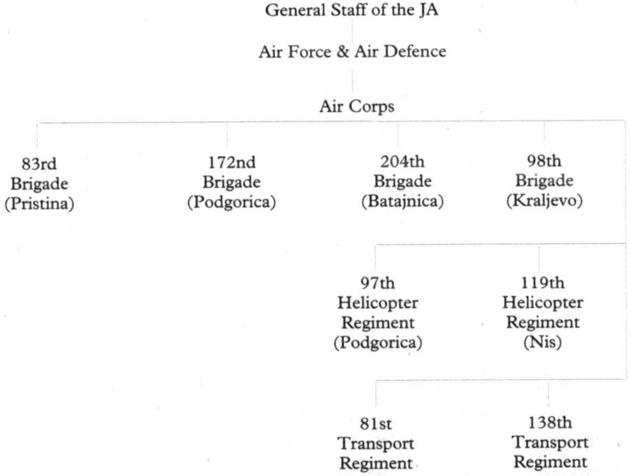

Strategic Weapons

Yugoslavia has the capability to develop chemical weapons and the funding to acquire strategic weapons. However because of organisational problems this is not a priority. If a radical political stance was adopted, the possibility of artillery delivered chemical weapons being produced and used cannot be excluded.

The army has two SS-1b 'Scud' ballistic missile launchers in its inventory. Each launcher has 10 reloads. Yugoslavia has no nuclear weapons but does have access to radioactive material from its nuclear power plants. This material could again be used as a radioactive weapon. Belgrade claims not to have access to biological weapons but reports suggest the existence of research facilities for such weapons. CS, BZ, Sarin and mustard chemical agents have probably been produced.

The MUP

The total strength of the *Ministarstvo Unutrasnjih Poslova* (MUP) is estimated at 110,000 and the force is well-equipped and trained. A special anti-terrorist unit (ATJ) is based at Batajnica near Belgrade, with special police units (PJP) formed in all major cities. Their official role is listed as riot control but they were used in suppressing armed resistance in Kosovo.

The MUP consists of a number of company sized light infantry units equipped with infantry weapons and armoured vehicles. Under command of the Minister of the Interior there are also a number of specialised anti-terrorist units such as the Special Operations Unit (Red Berets) and SAJ "Commandos".

Paramilitary Units

Serbian paramilitary units were created to spread terror and spearhead the policy of eviction and massacre during wars in Croatia and Bosnia. Their total strength is estimated at 10,000. After the outbreak of violence in Kosovo in early 1998 the MUP allegedly incorporated known members of paramilitary units. No freelance operations were confirmed in Kosovo but ad-hoc units were created and came under direct MUP command.

Srpska Dobrovoljacka Garda (SDG) (Arkan's Tigers): the SDG is led by Zeljko 'Arkan' Raznjatovic. He was allegedly involved in the killings of Croatian émigrés in Western Europe during the previous communist regime. The International Criminal Tribunal for former Yugoslavia (ICTY) confirmed the existence of an indictment against Arkan for his actions in Croatia. Members fought in Croatia and Bosnia but became better known for numerous atrocities against unarmed civilians. The SDG is reportedly a well-armed and disciplined force. It operates in groups of about 20 to 40 men.

Srpski Cetnicki Pokret (SCP): the SCP was led by Vojislav Seselj and had 1,500 fighters. Affiliated with the Serbian Radical Party, it is ill-disciplined and has been accused of war crimes in Bosnia-Herzegovina. It is armed with infantry weapons, including anti-tank rockets.

A report, which leaked out in October 1998, indicated that SCP had units in several Serbian cities and that lists of 'traitors', mainly liberal intellectuals and political opponents, were prepared. The report alleged that three-man SCP groups are prepared to assassinate those 'traitors' if the order is issued. The order could come only from Seselj. SCP strength is currently estimated at over 3,000.

Srpska Garda: the acting leader of the Srpska Garda is currently Zvonko Osmajlic. The organisation is affiliated with the Serbian Renewal Movement (SPO) but has less than 200 fighters.

Beli Orlovi: Led by Dragoslav Bokan and Mirko Jovic. This group reportedly consisted of some 500 men armed with infantry weapons. They were responsible for several massacres of unarmed civilians in Croatia, Bosnia and were reported to be in Kosovo in early 1998. Bokan was arrested in 1997 and charged with common robbery, breaking and entering and was sentenced to six years in jail. His current whereabouts are uncertain.

Crna Ruka (Black Hand): This organisation takes its name from the same group that killed the then-ruling Serbian King Milan in 1903 for his pro-Western attitudes. They have claimed responsibility for several attacks in Kosovo in 1998-99. A group of computer hackers have attacked various Western and Albanian Internet sites under the name of Black Hand but they appear unrelated.

Montenegrin Patriots: pro-independence Montenegrin youths have begun organising themselves for the possibility that armed resistance to federal forces may become necessary. Groups centered on known local leaders and were closely associated with the Liberal Alliance of Montenegro (LSCG). Montenegrin police purged them of the most radical elements and promised the remaining ones they would be armed and put under police command if Montenegro decides on independence.

Border Guards

Yugoslavia's land borders and riverine frontiers are guarded and patrolled by Border Guard units, which are classified as standard military units and in peacetime include up to 60 per cent conscripts. The Border Guard force consists of ground troops and a number of seagoing and riverine patrol craft. The force is directly subordinate to the General Staff of the Army in Belgrade. In July 1998 the federal government extended the border belt, which is the direct responsibility of the Border Guards, from 100 m to 5 km.

Security Forces

Sluzba Drzavne Bezbednost (SDB): the SDB is the state security service. It is believed to have been reformed in Belgrade after being purged of non-Serbs in 1993.

Military-Security Service: the Military-Security Service is the counter-intelligence service of the VJ.

Formerly Kontraobavestajna Sluzba, or KOS, it is responsible for the control and monitoring of all military and civilian members of the armed forces. Its informers are found at every command echelon and in every unit of the VJ.

UCK Military Overview

The bulk of the financing of the UCK (*Ushtria Çlirimtare e Kosovës - Kosovo Liberation Army*) seems to originate from two sources: drug-related operations along the traditional Balkan smuggling routes, and from the 500,000 Kosovan Albanian settlers in the West. The Albanian language is very different from any other spoken in Europe, making the infiltration of Kosovan opposition groups difficult. The close-knit clan nature of Albanian society has also served to hamper infiltration and acted as a secure base for recruitment and support. Many recruits were former students arrested in the 1980s for their participation in the movement demanding a Republic of Kosovo. Long prison sentences and the inability to gain employment after their release radicalised students to the point were they were ready to lead the armed struggle.

Arms were procured from all sources but the single most important channel was from Kosovan Serbs. Belgrade distributed an estimated 75,000 rifles to the Serbian community in Kosovo so they could protect themselves. The Serbs were quite happy to sell their guns to the Albanians, relying on the might of the VJ to protect them. Kosovar Albanians are traditionally a people with a gun-culture. Every home can be expected to own or have access to small arms. Another important channel for arms was Albania itself. Looting of military depots put more than half a million small arms on the market in 1997. The price of a Kalashnikov in northern Albania was as low as US$100; in Kosovo it was double. Supplies started flowing across the mountains, initially in smaller groups but convoys grew to include 200 mountain ponies and a thousand men.

Initially the only heavier weapons the UCK had were early generation shoulder-launched anti-tank weapons and limited numbers of smaller-calibre mortars. Land-mines were barely used, not even for perimeter defence. However, this reflected the Albanians' heroic system of values where the only worthy way to fight is with a gun. In mid-1998 the UCK attacked the town of Orahovac, displaying an appalling level of tactical incompetence, lack of proper command and fighting discipline. UCK commanders did not use their mobility but defended roadblocks, canyons and mountain passes with no attempt at surprise or flanking actions.

UCK Training

The UCK used the winter of 1998-99 to establish a competent central command structure around a General Staff (*Shtabi i Përgjithshëm* - ShP) and divided Kosovo into operational zones. Initially there were six of them, but OZ No. 7 (Karadak) was added in February along the southern flank and the crucial communication with Macedonia through Kacanik gorge. The total number of fighters reached 30,000 in mid-June 1998 but a large number of those were just locals carrying guns in their own villages. Some 50 shoulder-launched AA missiles (mostly SA-7/14 family, but including several Stingers) found their way into the KLA arsenal. Small arms reflect the multitude of sources of procurement - the Kalashnikov family still predominates - but exotic weapons such as Barrett 0.50 in sniping rifles, Steyr AUG and Heckler & Koch G3 assault rifles have been sighted. There is limited night-vision equipment. Communications are still rudimentary, with satellite telephones forming the backbone of OZ HQs and field radios in short supply. In areas covered by cellular telephone networks mobile phones are used.

The implementation of the NATO-Yugoslav military agreement of June 1999 saw the withdrawal of VJ and paramilitary forces from Kosovo. UCK fighters swiftly moved to fill the vacuum occupying towns and villages throughout the province. KLA troops established check-points and acted like a new paramilitary police force. After securing their base of operations the KLA agreed to demilitarisation and handed many weapons over to KFOR troops. The process of demilitarisation includes a ban on the carrying and possession of automatic weapons; the storage of heavy weapons at sites checked and eventually controlled by KFOR; the closing of military positions, including check-points; and an end to the wearing of uniforms and military insignia. The UCK is highly aware of its responsibilities in the running of civilian affairs. Many UCK members have found their way into the new police force and civil administration bodies throughout Kosovo.

KOSOVO LIBERATION ARMY (USHTRIA ÇLIRIMTARE Ë KOSOVËS – UÇK)

General Staff (Shtabi i Përgjithshëm – ShP)

Known members:	**Known duties:**
Sylejman Selimi – 'Sultan'	Commander-in-Chief
LtCol Bislim Zyrapi	Chief-of-Staff
Azem Syla – 'Daja i madh' (Big Uncle)	Supply of arms to North Albania
Fatmir Limaj – 'Çeliku' (Steel)	Internal organisation
Hashim Thaçi – 'Gjarpëri' (Snake)	Policy
Jakup Krasniqi	Civil administration and spokesman
Xhavit Haliti – 'Zeka'	Financing & Co-ordination with Albania
Ramë Buja	Political Representative
Pleurat Sejdiu	Co-ordination with Western Europe
Shaban Shala	Public Information & Morale
Sokol Barë	Recruitment of refugees in N Albania
Rexhep Selimi	Inspector General of the KLA
Gani Koci	Co-ordination with NGOs, foreign organisations
Sokol Bashota	Deputy Head of Political Directorate
Adem Grabovci	Personnel
Maj Salih Veseli – 'Vetima' (Thunderflash)	Military Education

Operational sub-divisions

1st Operational Zone – Drenica

HQ:	Lausa (Llaush)
Commanding Officer:	Sami Lustaku
Deputy CO:	Bashkim Jashari
Assistant CO for Morale:	Hyzri Tallaj
111 Brigade 'Adem Jashari' (name unconfirmed)	CO: unknown
Special Commando unit (Njësia Commando)	CO: 'Magjupi' ('Gypsy')
112 Brigade 'Abedin Sokol Rexha' (name unconf)	CO: Murat Mehmeti (unconf.)
113 Brigade 'Mujë Krasniqi'	CO: Hysen Shabani Asst CO: Murat Mehmeti
114 Brigade 'Fehmi Lladrovci'	CO: Muharrem Gashi (unconf) Asst CO (Morale): Gani Koci
Officer Training Centre 'Hamëz Jashari' (Qëndra te aftësimit të oficirëve)	Location: Likoc CO: 'Murrizi'

2nd Operational Zone – Llap

HQ:	Lapastica (Llapashtica)
Commanding Officer:	Nuredin Ibishi – 'Remi'
Deputy CO:	Kadri Kastrati – 'Daja' (Uncle)
Assistant CO:	Cpt Naim Maloku

121 Brigade 'Shaban Shala'	CO: Haxhi Shala
	Asst. CO (Logistics) Naser Shala
1st Battalion 'Afrim Krasniqi'	CO: Skender Hoti
3rd Battalion 'Sadik Shala'	CO: Ajet Kastrati
122 Brigade 'Zahir Pajaziti'	CO: 'Lekë'
123 Brigade (name unknown)	CO: unknown
Officers Training Centre (unconfirmed)	

3rd Operational Zone – Dukagjini (full name: Rrafshi i Dukagjinit)

HQ:	Jablanica
Commanding Officer:	Ramush Haradinaj
Chief-of-Staff:	Prof Maxhun Çekaj
Assistant CO (Logistics):	Rustem Teta
131 Brigade 'Jusuf Gërvalla'	CO: Rustem Berisha
132 Brigade 'Myrtë Zeneli'	CO: Nazmi Ukësmajli
133 Brigade 'Ardian Krasniqi'	CO: 'Imrin'
134 Brigade 'Bedri Shala'	CO: Ismet Ahmeti
Officers Training Centre	CO: Shaban Dragaj

4th Operational Zone – Shala (full name: Shala ë Bajgores)

HQ:	Near Magura
Commanding Officer:	Rrahman Rama
141 Brigade 'Mehë Uka'	CO: unknown
142 Brigade 'Azem Galica' (name unconfirmed)	CO: unknown
143 Brigade (name unknown)	Deputy CO: 'Enver'

5th Operational Zone – Pashtriku

HQ:	Dragobilje and Ladrovac (Lladrovc)
Commanding Officer:	Tahir Sinani
Deputy CO:	Dr Sadik Halitjaha
151 Brigade	CO: Vellaznim Kryeziu
152 Brigade	CO: Unknown
153 Brigade	CO: Unknown
Officer Training Centre	Location: Kostrce

6th Operational Zone – Nerodime

HQ:	unknown
Commanding Officer:	Shukri Buja
161 Brigade 'Ahmed Kaqiku' (name unconf)	CO: Hajros Kurti – 'Bardhi'
162 Brigade 'Agim Bajrami'	CO: Unknown

7th Operational Zone – Karadak

HQ:	Unknown
Commanding Officer:	Unknown
171 Brigade 'Kadri Zeka'	CO: Unknown

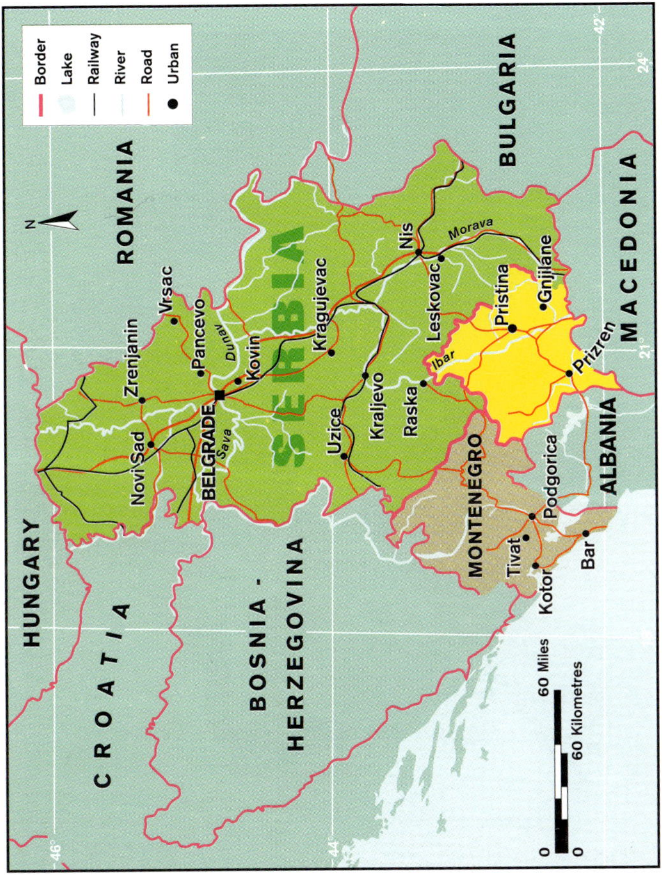

Border
Lake
Railway
River
Road
Urban
N
HUNGARY
ROMANIA
CROATIA
BOSNIA - HERZEGOVINA
SERBIA
BULGARIA
MACEDONIA
ALBANIA
MONTENEGRO
Novi Sad
Zrenjanin
Vrsac
Pancevo
BELGRADE
Kovin
Kragujevac
Uzice
Kraljevo
Raska
Nis
Leskovac
Pristina
Gnjilane
Prizren
Podgorica
Tivat
Kotor
Bar
Dunav
Sava
Ibar
Morava
0
60 Miles
0
60 Kilometres
46°
44°
42°
21°
24°

Bosnia

Photo: Antonio Prenda

Brigadier | Major General | Lieutenant General | General

2nd Lieutenant | Lieutenant | Captain | Major | Lieutenant Colonel | Colonel

Staff Sergeant | Sergeant 1st Class | 1st Sergeant | Sergeant Major | Regimental Sergeant Major

Private | Private 1st Class | Corporal | Sergeant

BOSNIA-HERCEGOVINA BiH

FEDERATION FLAG

Croatia

Photo: Yves Debay

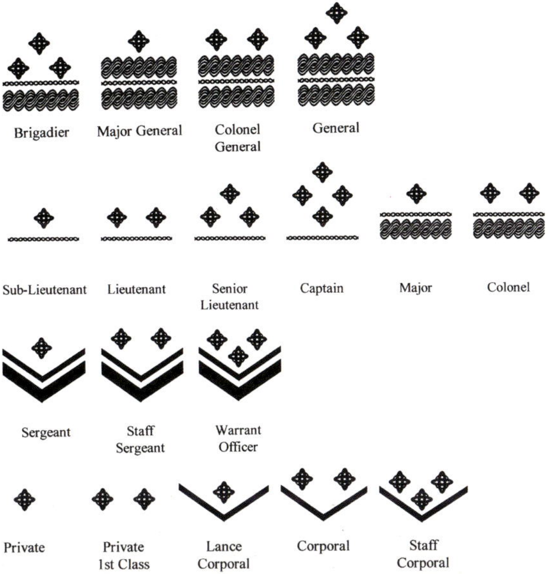
Brigadier
Major General
Colonel General
General
Sub-Lieutenant
Lieutenant
Senior Lieutenant
Captain
Major
Colonel
Sergeant
Staff Sergeant
Warrant Officer
Private
Private 1st Class
Lance Corporal
Corporal
Staff Corporal

Macedonia

Photo: Yves Debay

Slovenia

Photo: SFOR PIO

VRS

Photo: SFOR/PIO

VRS/VJ JACKET RANKS

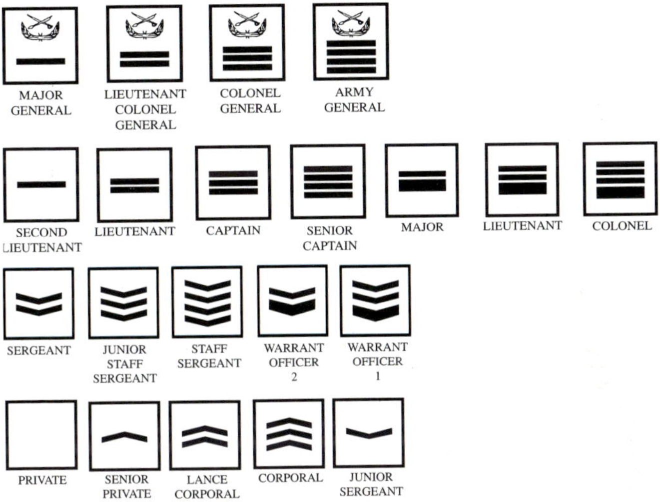

Yugoslavia/VJ

Photo: Paul Beaver

VRS/VJ SHOULDER BOARDS

Yugoslav MUP

Photo: PA

Bokan's Eagles

Photo: Yves Debay

UCK (KLA)

Photo: Yves Debay

Photo: Yves Debay

Albania

Photo: SFOR PIO

Photo: SFOR PIO

Belgium

Photo: SFOR PIO

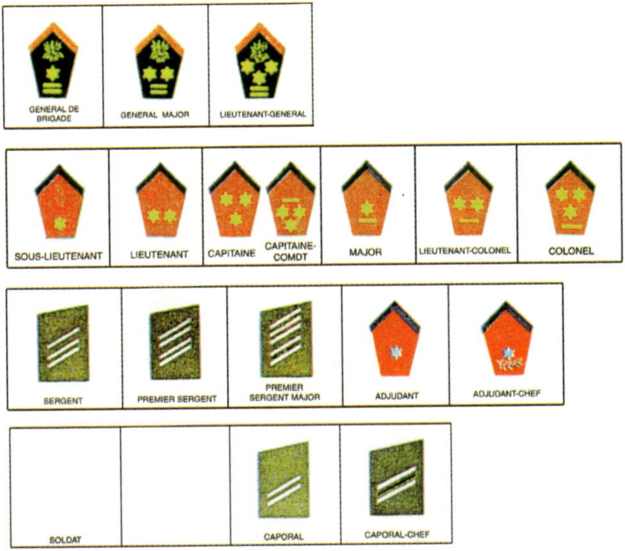
GENERAL DE BRIGADE
GENERAL MAJOR
LIEUTENANT-GENERAL
SOUS-LIEUTENANT
LIEUTENANT
CAPITAINE
CAPITAINE-COMDT
MAJOR
LIEUTENANT-COLONEL
COLONEL
SERGENT
PREMIER SERGENT
PREMIER SERGENT MAJOR
ADJUDANT
ADJUDANT-CHEF
SOLDAT
CAPORAL
CAPORAL-CHEF

Canada

Photo: SFOR PIO

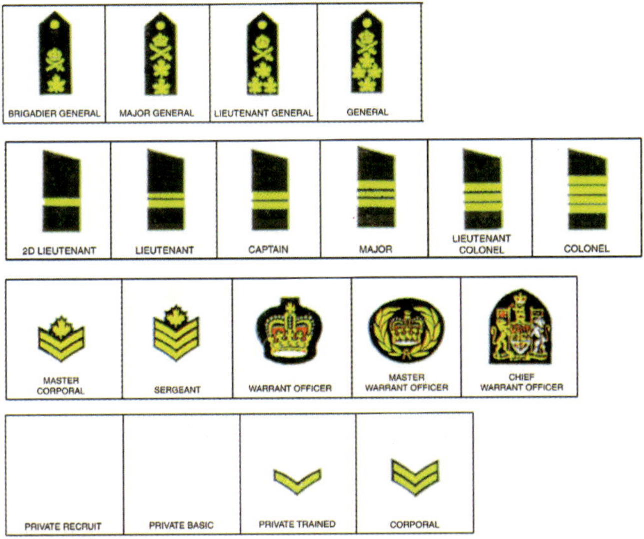
BRIGADIER GENERAL
MAJOR GENERAL
LIEUTENANT GENERAL
GENERAL
2D LIEUTENANT
LIEUTENANT
CAPTAIN
MAJOR
LIEUTENANT COLONEL
COLONEL
MASTER CORPORAL
SERGEANT
WARRANT OFFICER
MASTER WARRANT OFFICER
CHIEF WARRANT OFFICER
PRIVATE RECRUIT
PRIVATE BASIC
PRIVATE TRAINED
CORPORAL

Denmark

Photo: SFOR PIO

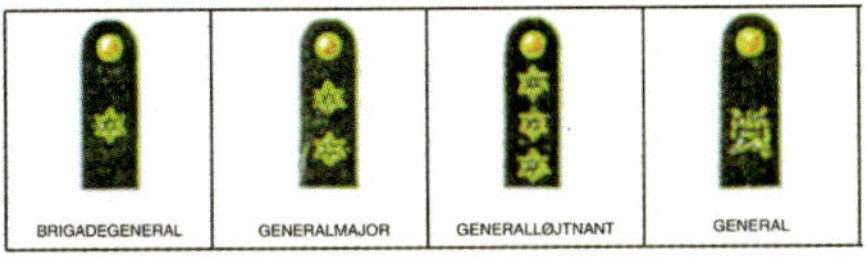
BRIGADEGENERAL
GENERALMAJOR
GENERALLØJTNANT
GENERAL

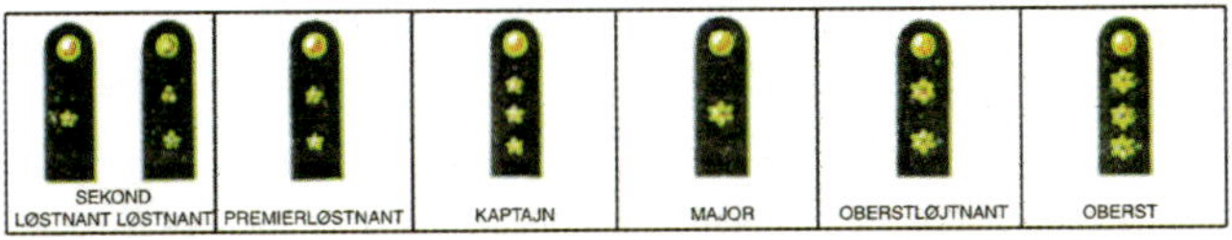
SEKOND
LØSTNANT LØSTNANT
PREMIERLØSTNANT
KAPTAJN
MAJOR
OBERSTLØJTNANT
OBERST

CONSCRIPT CAREER
SERGENT
OVERSERGENT
SENIORSERGENT 2
SENIORSERGENT 1

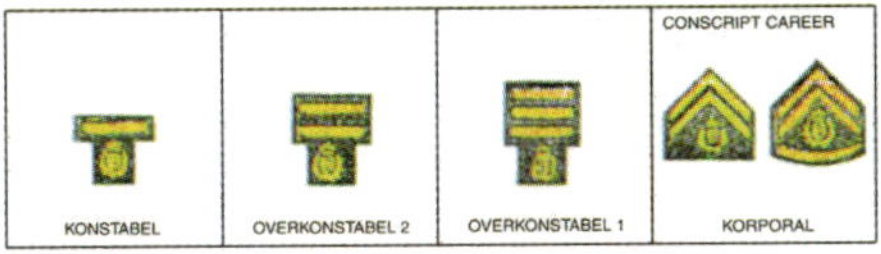
KONSTABEL
OVERKONSTABEL 2
OVERKONSTABEL 1
CONSCRIPT CAREER
KORPORAL

France

Photo: SFOR PIO

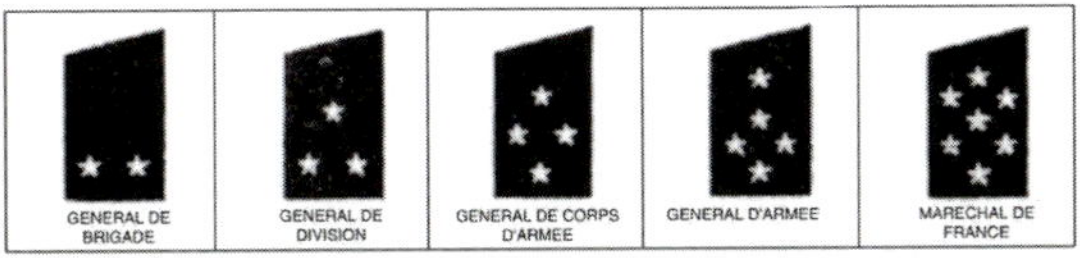
GENERAL DE BRIGADE
GENERAL DE DIVISION
GENERAL DE CORPS D'ARMEE
GENERAL D'ARMEE
MARECHAL DE FRANCE

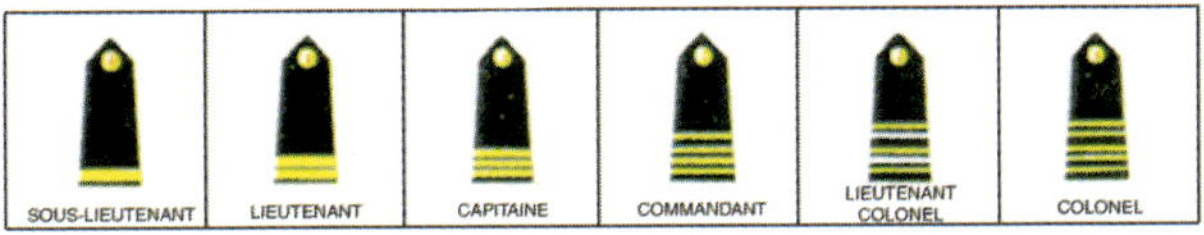
SOUS-LIEUTENANT
LIEUTENANT
CAPITAINE
COMMANDANT
LIEUTENANT COLONEL
COLONEL

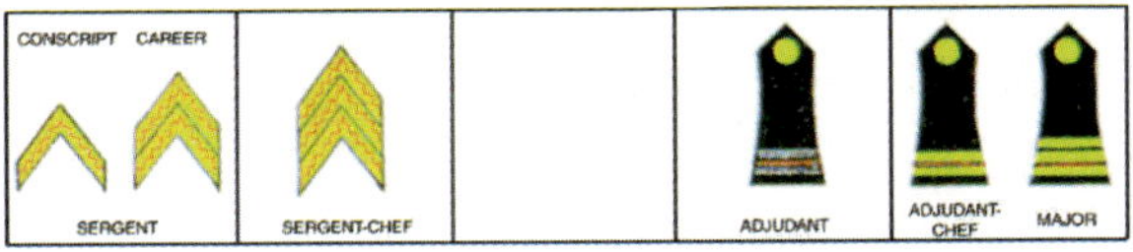
CONSCRIPT
CAREER
SERGENT
SERGENT-CHEF
ADJUDANT
ADJUDANT-CHEF
MAJOR

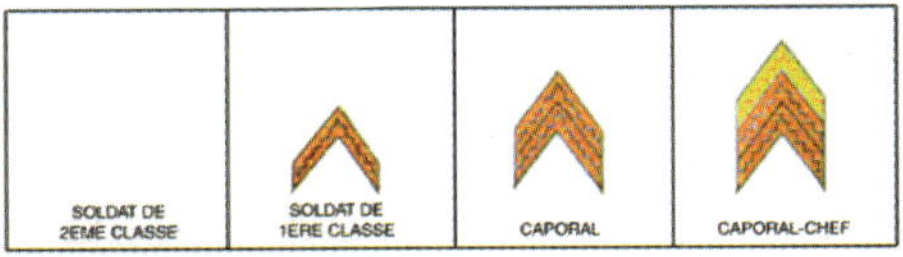
SOLDAT DE 2EME CLASSE
SOLDAT DE 1ERE CLASSE
CAPORAL
CAPORAL-CHEF

Germany

Photo: Yves Debay

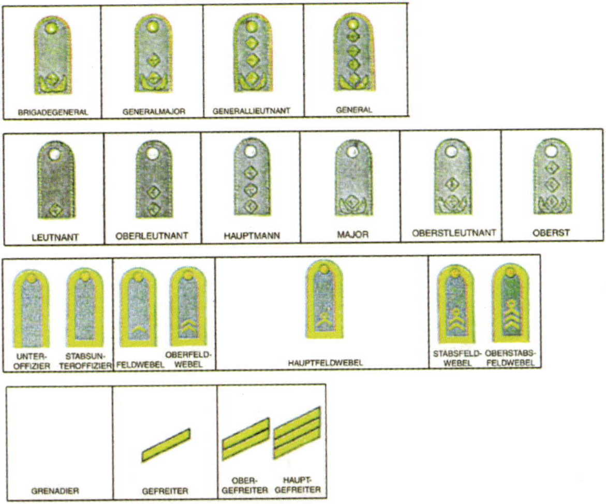
BRIGADEGENERAL
GENERALMAJOR
GENERALLIEUTNANT
GENERAL
LEUTNANT
OBERLEUTNANT
HAUPTMANN
MAJOR
OBERSTLEUTNANT
OBERST
UNTER-OFFIZIER
STABSUN-TEROFFIZIER
FELDWEBEL
OBERFELD-WEBEL
HAUPTFELDWEBEL
STABSFELD-WEBEL
OBERSTABS-FELDWEBEL
GRENADIER
GEFREITER
OBER-GEFREITER
HAUPT-GEFREITER

Greece

Photo: SFOR PIO

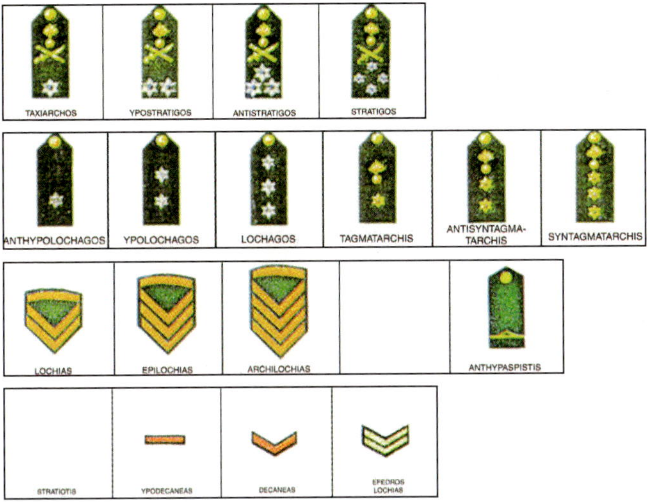
TAXIARCHOS
YPOSTRATIGOS
ANTISTRATIGOS
STRATIGOS
ANTHYPOLOCHAGOS
YPOLOCHAGOS
LOCHAGOS
TAGMATARCHIS
ANTISYNTAGMA-TARCHIS
SYNTAGMATARCHIS
LOCHIAS
EPILOCHIAS
ARCHILOCHIAS
ANTHYPASPISTIS
STRATIOTIS
YPODECANEAS
DECANEAS
EFEDROS LOCHIAS

Italy

Photo: SFOR PIO

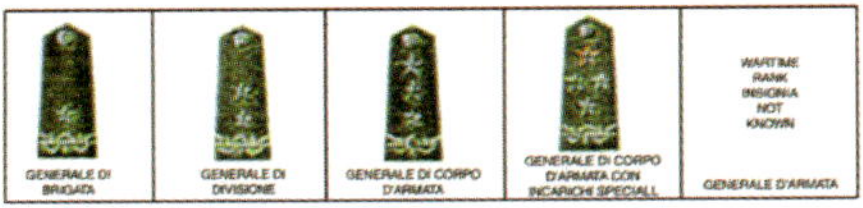
GENERALE DI BRIGATA
GENERALE DI DIVISIONE
GENERALE DI CORPO D'ARMATA
GENERALE DI CORPO D'ARMATA CON INCARICHI SPECIALL
WARTIME RANK INSIGNIA NOT KNOWN
GENERALE D'ARMATA

SOTTOTENENTE
TENENTE
CAPITANO
PRIMO CAPITANO
MAGGIORE
TENENTE COLONNELLO
COLONNELLO
COLONNELLO COMANDANTE DI CORPO

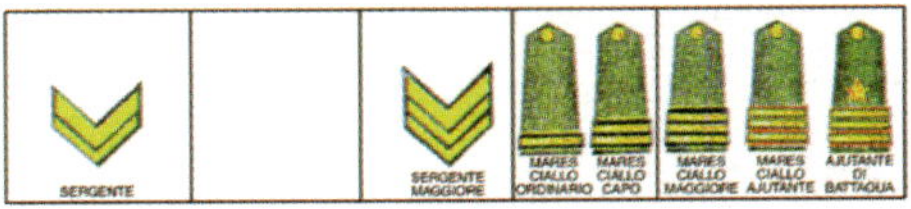
SERGENTE
SERGENTE MAGGIORE
MARES CIALLO ORDINARIO
MARES CIALLO CAPO
MARES CIALLO MAGGIORE
MARES CIALLO AJUTANTE
AJUTANTE DI BATTAGLIA

SOLDATO
CAPORALE
CAPORALE MAGGIORE

Netherlands

Photo: SFOR PIO

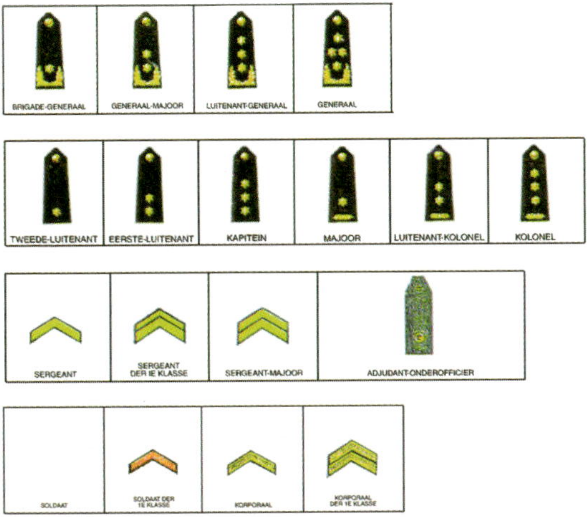
BRIGADE-GENERAAL
GENERAAL-MAJOOR
LUITENANT-GENERAAL
GENERAAL
TWEEDE-LUITENANT
EERSTE-LUITENANT
KAPITEIN
MAJOOR
LUITENANT-KOLONEL
KOLONEL
SERGEANT
SERGEANT DER 1E KLASSE
SERGEANT-MAJOOR
ADJUDANT-ONDEROFFICIER
SOLDAAT
SOLDAAT DER 1E KLASSE
KORPORAAL
KORPORAAL DER 1E KLASSE

Norway

Photo: SFOR PIO

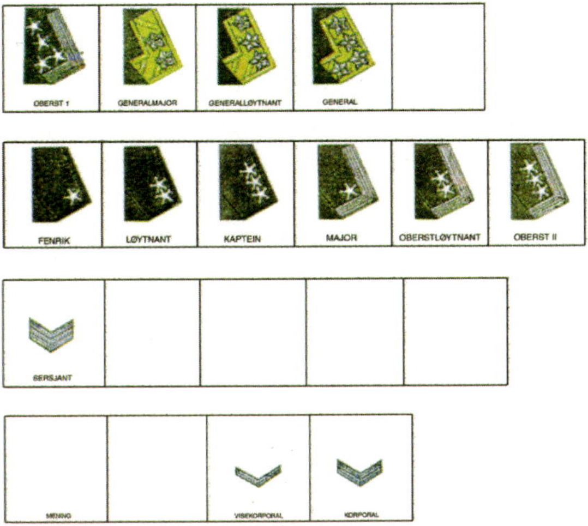
OBERST I
GENERALMAJOR
GENERALLØYTNANT
GENERAL
FENRIK
LØYTNANT
KAPTEIN
MAJOR
OBERSTLØYTNANT
OBERST II
SERSJANT
MENING
VISEKORPORAL
KORPORAL

Russia

Photo: SFOR PIO

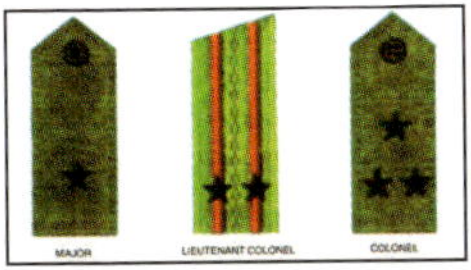
MAJOR
LIEUTENANT COLONEL
COLONEL

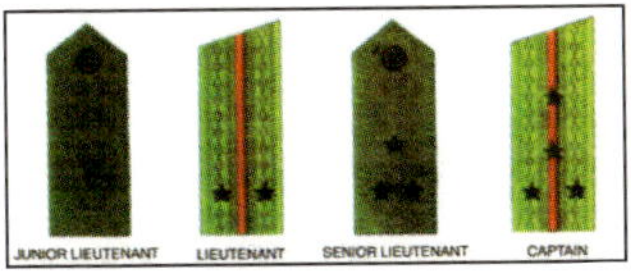
JUNIOR LIEUTENANT
LIEUTENANT
SENIOR LIEUTENANT
CAPTAIN

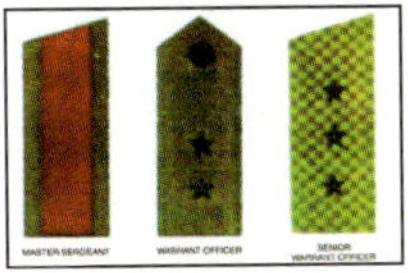
MASTER SERGEANT
WARRANT OFFICER
SENIOR WARRANT OFFICER

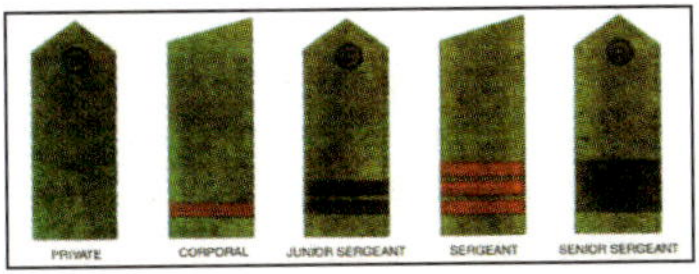
PRIVATE
CORPORAL
JUNIOR SERGEANT
SERGEANT
SENIOR SERGEANT

Spain

Photo: SFOR PIO

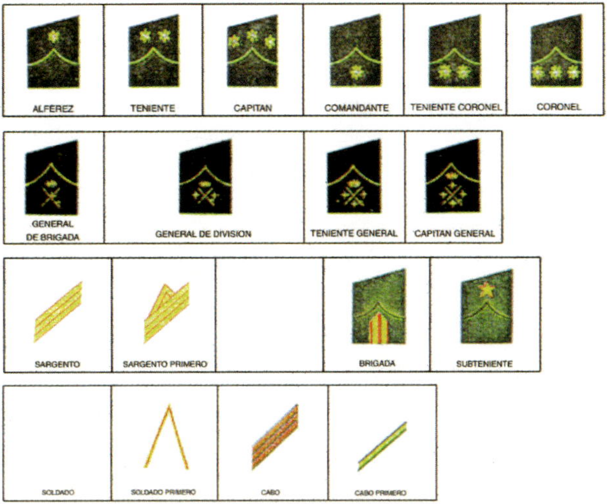
ALFEREZ
TENIENTE
CAPITAN
COMANDANTE
TENIENTE CORONEL
CORONEL
GENERAL DE BRIGADA
GENERAL DE DIVISION
TENIENTE GENERAL
CAPITAN GENERAL
SARGENTO
SARGENTO PRIMERO
BRIGADA
SUBTENIENTE
SOLDADO
SOLDADO PRIMERO
CABO
CABO PRIMERO

Sweden

Photo: SFOR PIO

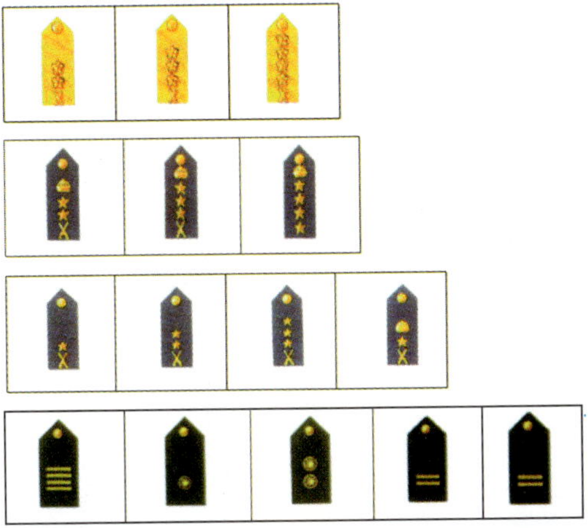

Turkey

Photo: SFOR PIO

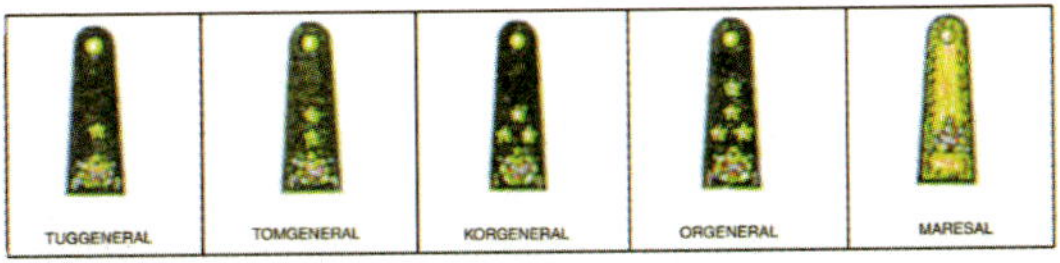
TUGGENERAL
TOMGENERAL
KORGENERAL
ORGENERAL
MARESAL

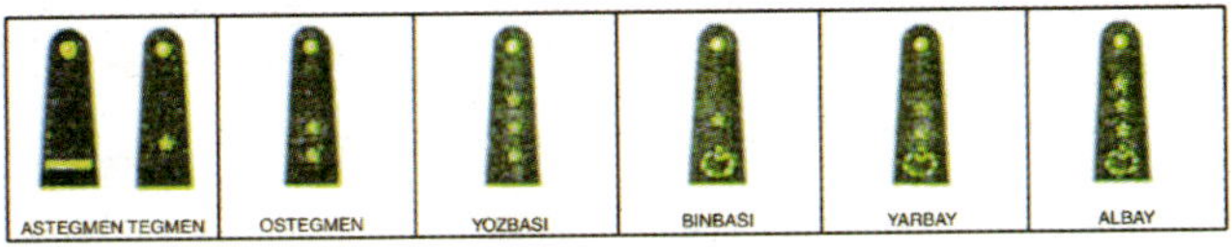
ASTEGMEN TEGMEN
OSTEGMEN
YOZBASI
BINBASI
YARBAY
ALBAY

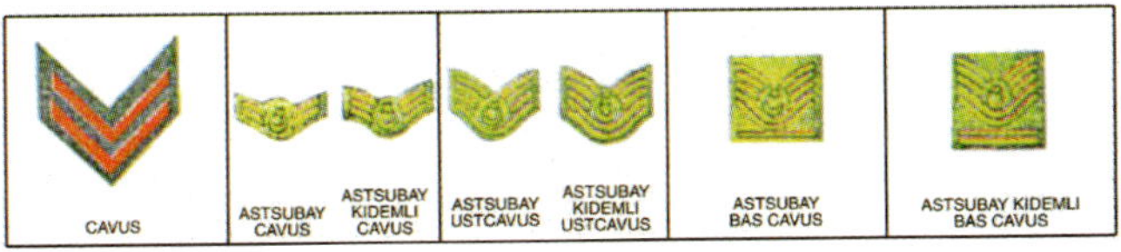
CAVUS
ASTSUBAY CAVUS
ASTSUBAY KIDEMLI CAVUS
ASTSUBAY USTCAVUS
ASTSUBAY KIDEMLI USTCAVUS
ASTSUBAY BAS CAVUS
ASTSUBAY KIDEMLI BAS CAVUS

ER
ONBASI

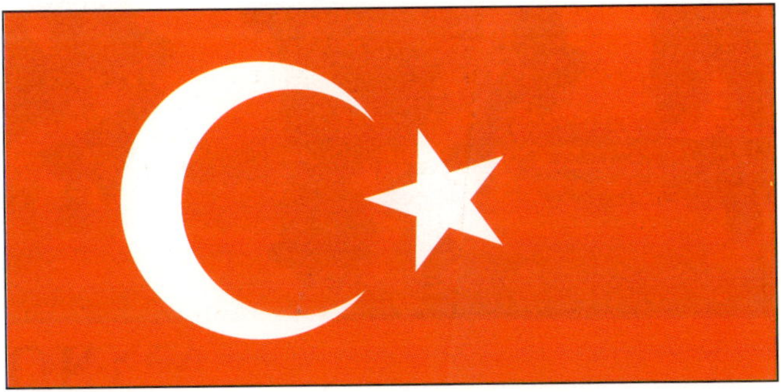

UK

Photo: Paul Beaver

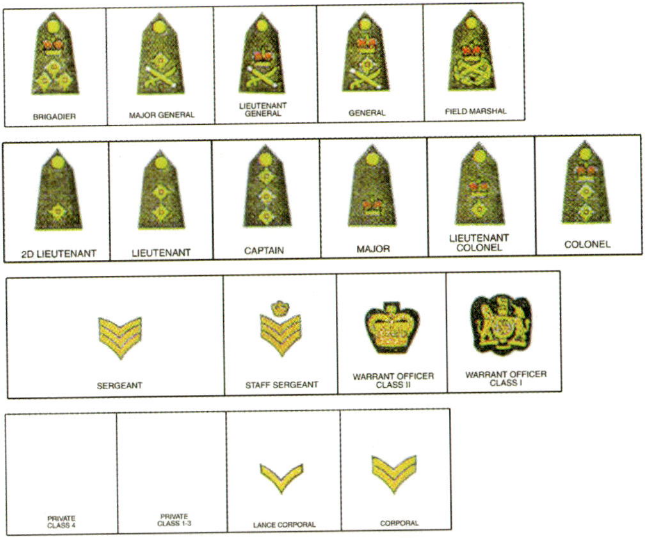
BRIGADIER
MAJOR GENERAL
LIEUTENANT GENERAL
GENERAL
FIELD MARSHAL
2D LIEUTENANT
LIEUTENANT
CAPTAIN
MAJOR
LIEUTENANT COLONEL
COLONEL
SERGEANT
STAFF SERGEANT
WARRANT OFFICER CLASS II
WARRANT OFFICER CLASS I
PRIVATE CLASS 4
PRIVATE CLASS 1-3
LANCE CORPORAL
CORPORAL

USA

Photo: SFOR PIO

2D LIEUTENANT
1ST LIEUTENANT
CAPTAIN
MAJOR
LIEUTENANT COLONEL
COLONEL
BRIGADIER GENERAL
MAJOR GENERAL
LIEUTENANT GENERAL
GENERAL
GENERAL OF THE ARMY
SERGEANT
STAFF SERGEANT
SERGEANT FIRST CLASS
MASTER SERGEANT
FIRST SERGEANT
SERGEANT MAJOR
COMMAND SERGEANT MAJOR
SERGEANT MAJOR OF THE ARMY
BASIC PRIVATE
PRIVATE
PRIVATE 1ST CLASS
CORPORAL

Argentina

Photo: SFOR PIO

Austria

Photo: SFOR PIO

Bulgaria

Photo: SFOR PIO

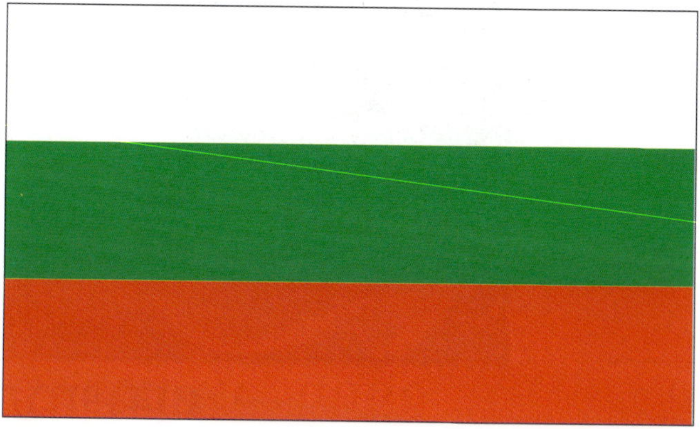

Czech Republic

Photo: SFOR PIO

Estonia

Photo: SFOR PIO

Finland

Photo: SFOR PIO

Hungary

Photo: SFOR PIO

Latvia

Photo: SFOR PIO

Lithuania

Photo: SFOR PIO

Morocco

Photo: SFOR PIO

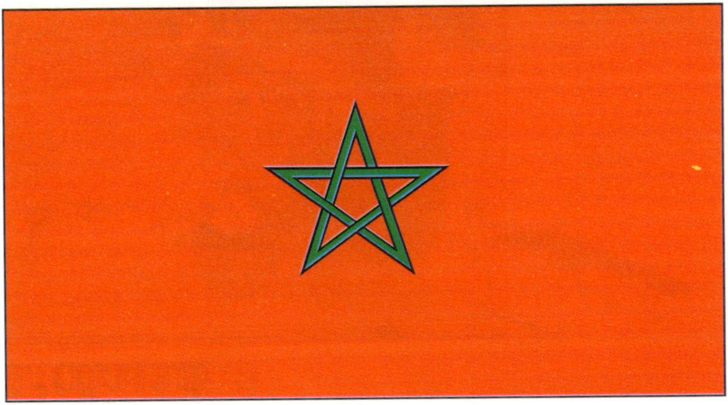

Poland

Photo: SFOR PIO

Portugal

Photo: SFOR PIO

Romania

Photo: SFOR PIO

Slovakia

Photo: SFOR PIO

UAE

Photo: Romeo Balencourt

Ukraine

Photo: SFOR PIO

NOTES

FORMER YUGOSLAV FORCES

NOTES

G-2 Galeb (Seagull)

Country of origin: Yugoslavia
Type: advanced trainer/ground attack aircraft
Used by: Republic of Srpska; Yugoslavia
Crew: 2 pilots
Armament: two 12.7 mm machine guns; bombs; rockets; bomblet dispensers
Recognition features: low/straight wing; wingtip fuel tanks; small intakes alongside cockpit
Length: 10.34 m **Wingspan**: 10.47 m

G-4 Super Galeb (Seagull)

Country of origin: Yugoslavia
Type: advanced trainer/ground attack aircraft
Used by: Bosnia-Herzegovina; Yugoslavia
Crew: 2 pilots
Armament: one ventral 23 mm cannon pod; IR AAMs; Maverick; cluster bombs; bombs; bomblet dispensers; rockets
Recognition features: low/swept wing; curved spine; ventral tailfin
Length: 12.25 m **Wingspan**: 9.88 m

J-1 Jastreb (Hawk)

Photo: Richard Strickland

Country of origin: Yugoslavia
Type: ground attack/reconnaissance aircraft
Used by: Republic of Srpska; Yugoslavia
Crew: 1 pilot
Armament: three 12.7 mm machine guns; bombs; bomblet dispensers; rockets
Recognition features: low/straight wing; wingtip tanks; single cockpit
Length: 10.88 m **Wingspan**: 11.68 m

J-22 Orao (Eagle)

Country of origin: Romania/Yugoslavia
Type: ground attack fighter/reconnaissance aircraft
Used by: Republic of Srpska; Yugoslavia
Crew: 1 pilot
Armament: two twin 23 mm cannons; Maverick; cluster bombs; bombs; napalm; rockets
Recognition features: high/swept wing; sharp pointed nose; fuselage tapers towards rear
Length: 14.9 m **Wingspan**: 9.3 m
Notes: two-seat versions also used in ground attack and reconnaissance roles.

An-2 Colt

Photo: Yves Debay

Country of origin: Ukraine
Type: light transport
Used by: Croatia; Yugoslavia
Crew: 1 pilot
Payload: 1,500 kg or 10 passengers
Recognition features: straight/biplane wings of unequal length; single rotary engine
Length: 12.95 m **Wingspan**: 18.18 m

UTVA-66

Country of origin: Yugoslavia
Type: light observation/transport
Used by: Bosnia-Herzegovina; Croatia; Yugoslavia
Crew: 1 pilot
Payload: 3 passengers
Recognition features: high/straight wing; single propeller; fixed landing gear
Length: 8.38 m **Wingspan**: 11.4 m

M10/36

Photo: Richard Strickland

Country of origin: USA
Type: tank destroyer
Used by: Yugoslavia
Crew: 5
Armament: 90 mm (main); 7.62 mm (bow); 12.7 mm (anti-aircraft)
Recognition features: six roadwheels in three bogies; sloped hull sides; semi-circular gun mount; open turret
Combat weight: 30,840 kg
Length: 6.27 m **Width** 2.55 m **Height**: 2.66 m

M18

Photo: Richard Strickland

Country of origin: USA
Type: tank destroyer
Used by: Yugoslavia
Crew: 5
Armament: 76 mm (main); 12.7 mm (anti-aircraft)
Recognition features: five large roadwheels; high sloped glacis; open turret
Combat weight: 17,036 kg
Length: 5.28 m **Width:** 2.79 m **Height**: 2.36 m

M47

Country of origin: USA
Type: medium tank
Used by: Yugoslavia
Crew: 5
Armament: 90 mm (main); 7.62 mm (coaxial); 7.62 mm (bow); 12.7 mm (anti-aircraft)
Recognition features: six small roadwheels; three return rollers; large turret bustle; bow machine gun
Combat weight: 46,170 kg
Length: 6.03 m **Width:** 3.51 m **Height**: 2.95 m

M-84

Photo: Paul Beaver

Country of origin: Croatia/Yugoslavia
Type: main battle tank
Used by: Croatia; Slovenia; Yugoslavia
Crew: 3
Armament: 125 mm 2A46 (main); 7.62 mm (coaxial); 12.7 mm (anti-aircraft)
Recognition features: six large roadwheels; V-shaped splash guard; wind sensor periscope over barrel
Combat weight: 42,000 kg
Length: 6.86 m **Width:** 3.57 m **Height**: 2.19 m

T-55

Photo: Paul Beaver

Country of origin: Russia
Type: main battle tank
Used by: Bosnia-Herzegovina; Croatia; Slovenia; Yugoslavia
Crew: 4
Armament: 100 mm (main); 7.62 mm (coaxial); 12.7 mm (Anti-Aircraft)
Recognition features: five roadwheels, prominent gap between first and second; fume extractor at end of barrel; round domed turret
Combat weight: 36,000 kg
Length: 6.20 m **Width:** 3.27 m **Height**: 2.35 m

AML-90

Photo: Antonio Prenda

Country of origin: France
Type: light armoured car
Used by: Bosnia-Herzegovina
Crew: 3
Armament: 90 mm (main); 7.62 mm (coaxial)
Recognition features: 4 x 4 roadwheels; D-shaped crew door; low turret with long main armament
Combat weight: 5,500 kg
Length: 3.79 m **Width:** 1.97 m **Height**: 1.38 m

BTR-50

Country of origin: Russia
Type: armoured personnel carrier
Used by: Slovenia; Yugoslavia
Crew: 2 + 20
Armament: 7.62 mm
Recognition features: six equally spaced small roadwheels; high frontal glacis; square forward troop compartment; roof hatches
Combat weight: 14,200 kg
Length 7.08 m **Width:** 3.14 m **Height**: 1.97 m

M-60P

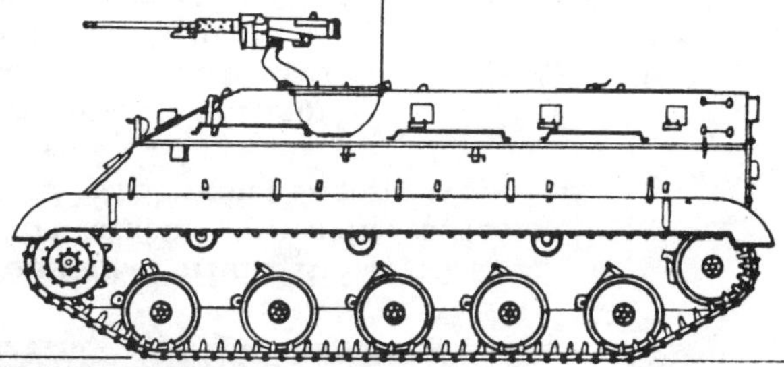

Country of origin: Yugoslavia
Type: armoured personnel carrier
Used by: Croatia; Yugoslavia
Crew: 3 + 10
Armament: 12.7 mm M2 (anti-aircraft); 7.92 mm (bow)
Recognition features: five small roadwheels; large sloped frontal glacis; square body
Combat weight: 11,000 kg
Length: 5.02 m **Width:** 2.77 m **Height**: 3.51 m (MG at max elevation)

M-80

Country of origin: Yugoslavia
Type: mechanised infantry combat vehicle
Used by: Bosnia-Herzegovina; Croatia; Macedonia; Slovenia; Yugoslavia
Crew: 3 + 7
Armament: 20 mm (main); 7.62 mm (coaxial); twin 'Sagger' ATGW launcher
Recognition features: five small equally spaced roadwheels; small round central turret; long sloped frontal glacis
Combat weight: 13,700 kg
Length: 6.4 m **Width:** 2.59 m **Height**: 1.8 m (to hull roof)

BOV-3

Photo: Roderick de Norman

Country of origin: Yugoslavia
Type: wheeled armoured personnel carrier; self-propelled anti-aircraft gun; ATGW carrier
Used by: Croatia; Slovenia; Yugoslavia
Crew: 2 + 8
Armament: 7.62 mm (APC); triple 20 mm (SPAAG); AT-3 'Sagger' (ATGW)
Recognition features: 4 x 4 roadwheels; external magazines on 20 mm cannons; the APC has raised hull roof with bulletproof windscreen
Combat weight: 5,700 kg
Length: 5.70 m **Width:** 2.53 m **Height**: 2.33 m

BTR-152

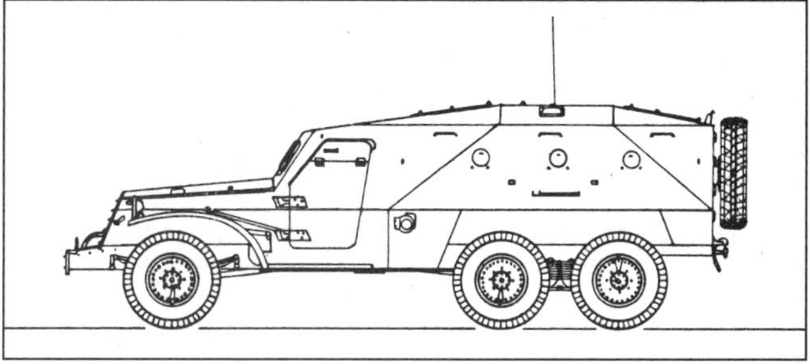

Country of origin: Russia
Type: wheeled armoured personnel carrier
Used by: Yugoslavia
Crew: 2 + 17
Armament: 7.62 mm machine gun
Recognition features: 6 x 6 roadwheels; conventional truck layout
Combat weight: 8,950 kg
Length: 6.55 m **Width:** 2.32 m **Height**: 2.36 m

LOV

Country of origin: Croatia
Type: wheeled armoured personnel carrier
Used by: Croatia
Crew: 2 + 10
Armament: 12.7 mm
Recognition features: 4 x 4 or 6 x 6 roadwheels; low open turret; raised driver's cab
Combat weight: 9,200 kg
Length: 5.89 m **Width:** 2.39 m **Height:** 1.98 m

M3 Panhard

Photo: Antonio Prenda

Country of origin: France
Type: wheeled armoured personnel carrier
Used by: Bosnia-Herzegovina
Crew: 2 + 10
Armament: 7.62 mm or 12.7 mm
Recognition features: 4 x 4 roadwheels; sharp angular nose; side doors under spare wheel
Combat weight: 6,100 kg
Length: 4.45 m **Width:** 2.4 m **Height**: 2 m

OT-64

Country of origin: Czech Republic/Poland
Type: armoured personnel carrier
Used by: Yugoslavia
Crew: 2 + 18
Armament: 14.5 mm (main); 7.62 mm (coaxial)
Recognition features: 8 x 8 roadwheels, large gap between the second and third; central conical turret
Combat weight: 14,300 kg
Length: 7.44 m **Width:** 2.55 m **Height**: 2.06 m

76 mm M48

Country of origin: Yugoslavia
Type: mountain gun
Used by: Yugoslavia; Bosnia-Herzegovina and Croatia (unconfirmed users)
Crew: 6
Maximum range: 8,750 m
Rate of fire: 25 rds/min
Recognition features: short barrel with large muzzle break; armoured blast shield
Barrel length: 1.178 m

76 mm M1942

Country of origin: Russia
Type: field gun
Used by: Yugoslavia
Crew: 7
Maximum range: 13,290 m
Rate of fire: 15-20 rds/min (initial 6 sustained)
Recognition features: armoured blast shield; recoil dampers above and below gun
Barrel length: 3.45 m

85 mm M1944 (D-44)

Photo: Jaroslaw Cislak

Country of origin: Russia
Type: field gun
Used by: Yugoslavia
Crew: 8
Maximum range: 15,650 m
Rate of fire: 15-20 rds/min
Recognition features: long tapered barrel; double baffle muzzle brake; scalloped blast shield
Barrel length: 4.69 m (overall)

100 mm T-12

Country of origin: Russia
Type: anti-tank gun
Used by: Croatia; Yugoslavia
Crew: 6
Maximum range: 8,200 m (HE indirect); 5,955 m (HEAT direct); 3,000 m (APFSDS direct)
Rate of fire: 14 rds/min
Recognition features: very long slim stepped barrel; pepperpot muzzle break; blast shield
Length: 9.48 m (travelling)

100 mm M87 Topaz

Country of origin: Yugoslavia
Type: anti-tank gun
Used by: Yugoslavia
Crew: 5-7
Maximum range: 7,800 m (HE); 2,230 m (APFSDS-T); 1,200 m (HEAT-T)
Rate of fire: 14 rds/min (max); 8 rds/min (normal)
Recognition features: recoil damper above barrel; blast shield; towing hoop on muzzle break
Barrel length: 6.3 m

105 mm M18

Photo: Christopher F. Foss

Country of origin: Germany
Type: howitzer
Used by: Yugoslavia
Crew: 8
Maximum range: 10,675 m
Rate of fire: 6-8 rds/min
Recognition features: recoil dampers staggered above and below barrel; large eight-spoke wheels
Barrel length: 2.94 m

105 mm M56

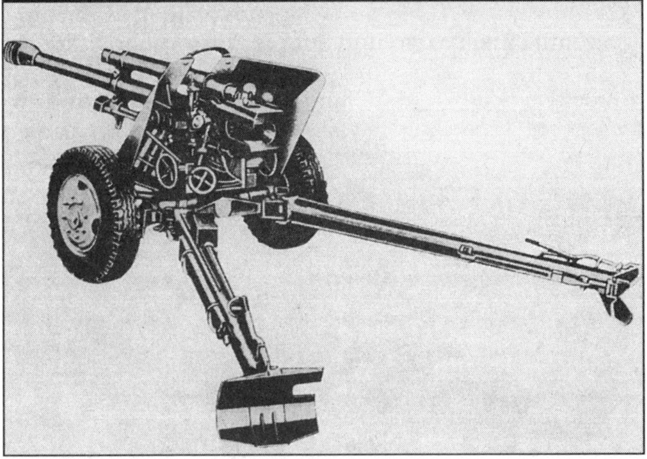

Country of origin: Yugoslavia
Type: howitzer
Used by: Yugoslavia
Crew: 7
Maximum range: 13,000 m
Rate of fire: 16 rds/min
Recognition features: muzzle break; recoil dampers above and below barrel; curved blast shield
Barrel length: 3.48 m

122 mm D-74

Country of origin: Russia
Type: field gun
Used by: Yugoslavia
Crew: 10
Maximum range: 24,000 m
Rate of fire: 6-7 rds/min
Recognition features: long thin barrel; large muzzle break; small blast shield
Barrel length: 6.45 m

122 mm M-30

Country of origin: Russia
Type: howitzer
Used by: Croatia; Yugoslavia
Crew: 8
Maximum range: 11,800 m; 630 m (effective, HEAT)
Rate of fire: 5-6 rds/min
Recognition features: angled blast shield; recoil dampers above and below barrel
Barrel length: 2.8 m

130 mm M-46

Country of origin: Russia
Type: field gun
Used by: Bosnia; Croatia; Yugoslavia
Crew: 8

Rate of fire: 5-6 rds/min
Range: 27,150 m
Recognition features: very long barrel; short recoil drapes; small blast shield
Barrel length: 7.6 m

152 mm M-84 (D-20)

Country of origin: Yugoslavia
Type: gun-howitzer
Used by: Bosnia-Herzegovnia; Yugoslavia
Crew: 9
Maximum range: 24,160 m; 27,000 m (with HE base-bleed projectile)
Rate of fire: 6 rds/min (max); 4 rds/min (normal)
Recognition features: thick barrel; large muzzle break; blast shield with curved top edge
Barrel length: 6.056 m
Notes: the M-84 is a Yugoslav-built copy of the D-20, capable of firing base-bleed ammunition.

155 mm M2

Country of origin: USA
Type: M-59 gun
Used by: Yugoslavia
Crew: 14
Maximum range: 22,000 m
Rate of fire: 2 rds/min
Recognition features: eight-wheel carriage; diagonal recoil dampers; long barrel
Barrel length: 7.036 m

155 mm M46/84

Country of origin: Yugoslavia
Type: converted gun
Used by: Yugoslavia
Crew: 8 + 1
Range: 30,300 m
Rate of fire: 6 rds/min (max); 4 rds/min (normal)
Recognition features: very long barrel; carriage has two auxiliary wheels
Barrel length: 6.97 m

155 mm M65

Country of origin: USA
Type: howitzer
Used by: Bosnia-Herzegovina; Croatia; Yugoslavia
Crew: 10
Maximum range: 14,955 m
Rate of fire: 3 rds/min
Recognition features: recoil damper above barrel; barrel slide beneath
Barrel length: 3.77 m

203 mm M1

Country of origin: USA
Type: howitzer
Used by: Yugoslavia
Crew: 14
Maximum range: 16,800 m
Rate of fire: 1 rd/min (max); 1 rd/2 min (sustained)
Recognition features: eight-wheel carriage; diagonal recoil dampers; short barrel
Barrel length: 5.14 m

70 mm M93A2 Heron

Country of origin: Croatia
Type: multiple rocket system
Used by: Croatia
Crew: 3-4
Number of barrels: 40
Maximum range: 8,100 m (M95 rocket system)
Recognition features: square box; two-wheel carriage
Length: 3.15 m **Width:** 1.85 m **Height:** 1.4 m

122 mm BM-21

Country of origin: Russia
Type: multiple rocket system
Used by: Bosnia; Croatia; Yugoslavia
Crew: 6
Number of barrels: 40
Maximum range: 20,000 m
Recognition features: 6 × 6 truck chassis; trainable tubular launcher
Length: 6.9 m **Width:** 2.5 m **Height:** 2.48 m

128 mm M-63 Plamen

Country of origin: Yugoslavia
Type: multiple rocket system
Used by: Bosnia-Herzegovina; Croatia; Macedonia; Slovenia; Yugoslavia
Crew: 7
Number of barrels: 1 to 32
Maximum range: 8,545 m
Recognition features: box body; two-wheel carriage; single-tube launcher has mortar base plate
Length: 3.62 m **Width:** 2.21 m **Height:** 1.27 m
Notes: a single-round 'Partizan' launcher was developed for use by commando and territorial defence units.

128 mm RAK-12/24

Country of origin: Croatia
Type: multiple rocket system
Used by: Croatia
Crew: 3-4
Number of barrels: 12
Maximum range: 8,500 m (M91 rocket); 13,000 m (M93 rocket)
Recognition features: 4 × 4 LOV chassis; cut away rear hull
Length: 5.89 m **Width:** 2.36 m

128 mm M-77 Oganj

Country of origin: Yugoslavia
Type: multiple rocket system
Used by: Bosnia-Herzegovina; Croatia; Yugoslavia
Crew: 5
Number of barrels: 32
Maximum range: 20,600 m
Recognition features: 6 × 6 truck chassis; trainable box and tube launcher; sliding tarpaulin cover
Length: 8.4 m **Width:** 2.99 m **Height:** 3.1 m

262 mm M-87 Orkan

Country of origin: Yugoslavia
Type: multiple rocket system
Used by: Bosnian Serb Army; Croatia; Yugoslavia
Crew: 5
Number of barrels: 12
Maximum range: 50,000 m
Recognition features: 8 × 8 truck chassis; anti-aircraft MG; sliding tarpaulin cover
Length: 9.00 m **Width:** 2.64 m **Height:** 3.84 m

FROG-7

Country of origin: Russia
Type: artillery rocket system
Used by: Yugoslavia
Crew: 7
Number of barrels: 1 missile
Maximum range: 65,000-70,000 m
Recognition features: 8 × 8 launch vehicle; middle wheels close together
Length: 10.69 m **Width:** 2.8 m **Height:** 3.35 m

20 mm M-55 A2

Country of origin: Yugoslavia
Type: anti-aircraft gun
Used by: Bosnia-Herzegovina; Croatia; Macedonia; Slovenia; Yugoslavia
Crew: 6
Ammunition: HEI-T; HE-T; HEI; HE; API; API-T; AP-T

Effective range: 2,500 m (horizontal); 2,000 m (vertical)
Maximum range: 5,500 m (horizontal); 4,000 m (vertical, under 80°)
Recognition features: three barrels; three-legged mount; drum magazines
Weight: 1,100 kg (with loaded drums); 970 kg (with empty drums)

20 mm M-75

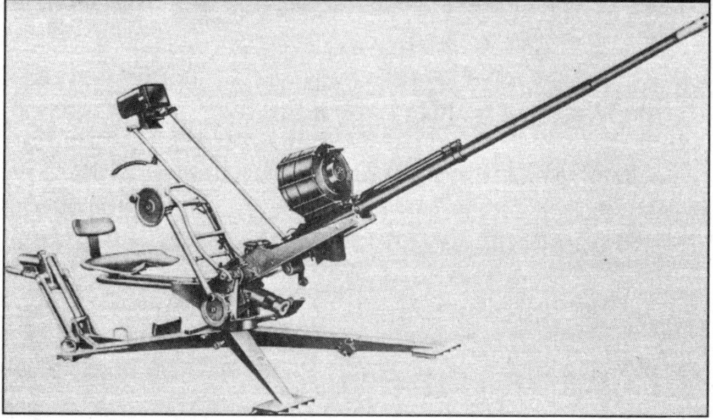

Country of origin: Yugoslavia
Type: anti-aircraft gun
Used by: Bosnia-Herzegovina; Croatia; Macedonia; Slovenia; Yugoslavia
Crew: 4-6
Ammunition: HEI-T; HE-T; HEI; HE; API; API-T; AP-T
Effective range: 2,000 m (aerial targets); 1,000 m plus (ground targets)
Maximum range: 5,500 m (horizontal); 4,000 m (vertical, under 80°)
Recognition features: single barrel; drum magazine
Weight: 260 kg

30 mm M53/153

Country of origin: Czech Republic
Type: anti-aircraft gun
Used by: Yugoslavia
Crew: 4
Ammunition: API; HEI
Effective range: 3,000 m (vertical)
Maximum range: 9,700 m (horizontal); 6,300 m (vertical)
Recognition features: 6 × 6 armoured truck chassis; twin gun mount at rear; large box magazines
Weight: 2,100 kg (travelling order); 1,750 kg (firing position)

37 mm M1939

Country of origin: Russia
Type: anti-aircraft gun
Used by: Albania; Yugoslavia
Crew: 8
Ammunition: FRAG-T9; AP-T
Effective range: 3,000 m (vertical)
Maximum range: 9,500 m (horizontal); 6,700 m (vertical)
Recognition features: single barrel; four-wheeled carriage; similar to the Bofors L/70 but has no shield
Weight: 2,100 kg

57 mm S-60

Country of origin: Russia
Type: anti-aircraft gun
Used by: Albania; Yugoslavia
Crew: 7
Ammunition: FRAG-T; APCT-T
Effective range: 6,000 m (vertical, carriage fire control); 4,000 m (with on-carriage fire control)
Maximum range: 12,000 m (horizontal); 8,800 m (vertical)
Recognition features: single barrel; narrow four-wheeled carriage
Weight: 4.39 m (overall)

ZSU-57-2

Country of origin: Russia
Type: twin 57 mm self-propelled anti-aircraft gun system
Used by: Bosnia-Herzegovnia; Yugoslavia
Crew: 6
Ammunition: FRAG-T; APC-T; HE-T
Maximum range: 12,000 m (horizontal); 8,800 m (vertical)
Recognition features: tracked vehicle; four road wheels; twin gun open turret
Weight: 28,100 kg

SA-2 Guideline

Country of origin: Russia
Type: low- to high-altitude surface-to-air missile system
Used by: Albania; Bosnia-Herzegovina; Yugoslavia
Crew (or launcher): single rail semi-fixed trainable
Maximum effective altitude: 22,000 m (SA-2a); 30,000 m (SA-2b/c/d/e/f)
Maximum effective range: 30,000 m (SA-2a); 34,000 m (SA-2b)
Recognition features: three sets of four wings, each set unequal in size
Weight: 2,280 kg

SA-3 Goa

Country of origin: Russia
Type: low- to medium-altitude surface-to-air missile system
Used by: Yugoslavia
Crew (or launcher): twin or quadruple rail semi-fixed trainable ground mount
Maximum effective altitude: 12,000 m (SA-3a); 18,000 m (SA-3b)
Maximum effective range: 22,000 m (SA-3a); 25,000 m (SA-3b)
Recognition features: two or four-round trainable launcher; 6 × 6 loading vehicle, carries two rounds
Weight: 639 kg (SA-3a); 641 kg (SA-3b)

SA-6 Gainful

Country of origin: Russia
Type: low- to medium-altitude surface-to-air missile system
Used by: Yugoslavia
Crew (or launcher): 3
Maximum effective altitude: 14,000 m
Maximum effective range: 24,000 m
Recognition features: armoured tracked carrier; six road wheels; three-round launcher
Weight: 599 kg

SA-9 Gaskin

Country of origin: Russia
Type: low altitude surface-to-air missile system
Used by: Croatia; Slovenia; Yugoslavia
Crew (or launcher): 3 (commander, gunner and driver)
Maximum effective altitude: 3,500 m (9M31); 6,100 m (9M31M)
Maximum effective range: 4,200 m (9M31); 8,000 m (9M31M) range increases to 11,000 m in tail chase against slow manoeuvring target
Recognition features: BRDM-2 carrier; folding four-round launcher
Weight: 32 kg (missile)

SA-11 Gadfly

Photo: Paul Jackson

Country of origin: Russia
Type: low- to high-altitude surface-to-air missile system
Used by: Yugoslavia
Maximum effective altitude: 22,000 m
Maximum effective range: 32,000 m
Recognition features: armoured tracked carrier; six roadwheels; four-round square faced launcher
Weight: 690 kg (9M38M1 missile)

SA-13 Gopher

Country of origin: Russia
Type: low-altitude surface-to-air missile system
Used by: Croatia
Crew (or launcher): 3 (commander, gunner and driver)
Maximum effective altitude: 3,500 m
Maximum effective range: 5,000 m
Recognition features: MTLB carrier; folding four-round launcher
Weight: 39.2 kg (9M37/9M37M); 42 kg (9M333)

7.62 mm Type 54

Country of origin: China
Type: recoil, semi-automatic pistol
Used by: Albania; Croatia; Yugoslavia
Ammunition: 7.62 × 25 mm 'P' cartridge (Type 51)
Range: 50 m
Feed: 8-round box magazine
Weight: 890 g (empty)

7.62 mm M57/70

Country of origin: Yugoslavia
Type: short recoil pistol
Used by: Bosnia-Herzegovina; Croatia; Yugoslavia
Ammunition: 7.62 × 25 mm
Range: 50 m
Feed: 9-round box magazine
Weight: approximately 900 g

0.357 Magnum

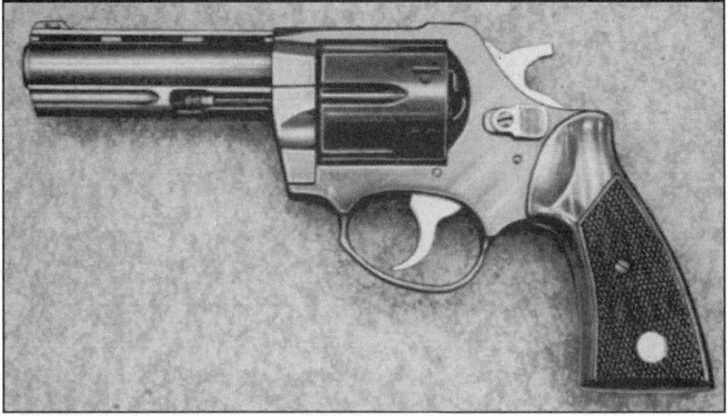

Country of origin: Yugoslavia
Type: Model 1983 double-action revolver
Used by: Yugoslav police
Ammunition: 0.357 Magnum
Range: 50 m
Feed: 6-round cylinder
Weight: 900 g (empty)

0.22 MGV-176

Country of origin: Slovenia
Type: standard blowback sub-machine gun
Used by: Slovenian special forces; Yugoslav paramilitaries
Ammunition: 0.22 long rifle
Range: 150 m
Feed: 176-round drum magazine
Weight: 2.88 kg (empty); 3.45 kg (loaded)

7.62 mm M56

Country of origin: Yugoslavia
Type: standard blowback sub-machine gun
Used by: Bosnia-Herzegovina; Croatia; UCK; Yugoslavia
Ammunition: 7.62 × 25 mm Type P Pistol or 7.63 mm Mauser
Range: 200 m
Feed: 35-round curved box magazine
Weight: 3 kg

7.65 mm Model 84

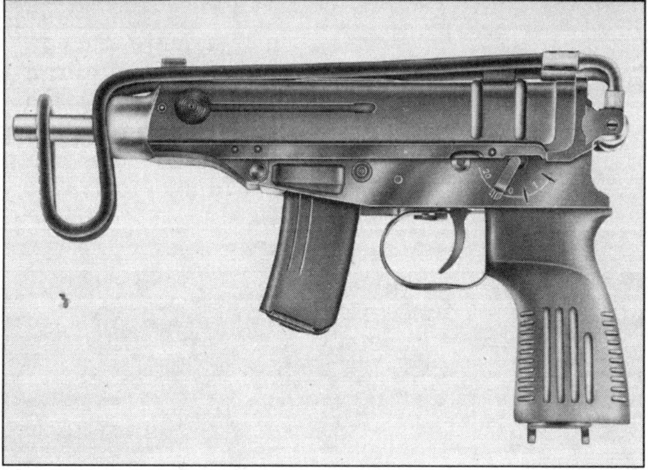

Country of origin: Yugoslavia
Type: machine pistol
Used by: Bosnia-Herzegovina; Croatia; Slovenia; UCK; Yugoslavia
Ammunition: 0.32 ACP (7.65 mm)
Range: 150 m (effective)
Feed: 10- or 20-round box magazine
Weight: 1.28 kg (empty, less magazine)

7.62 mm PPsH-41

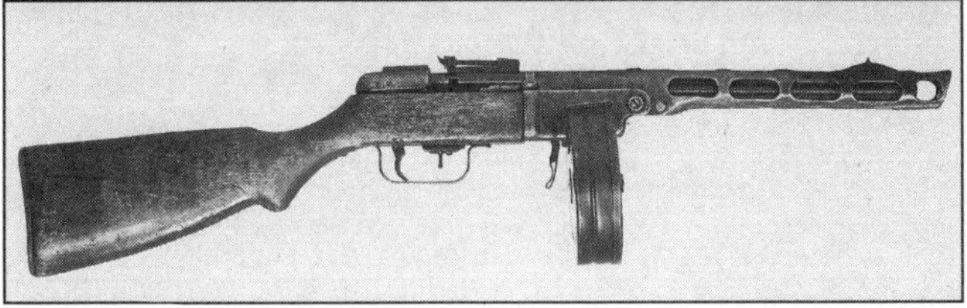

Country of origin: Russia
Type: sub-machine gun
Used by: Albania; UCK
Ammunition: 7.62 mm × 25 mm
Range: 200 m
Feed: 35-round box magazine, 71-round drum magazine
Weight: 3.5 kg

7.62 mm M59/66A1/SKS

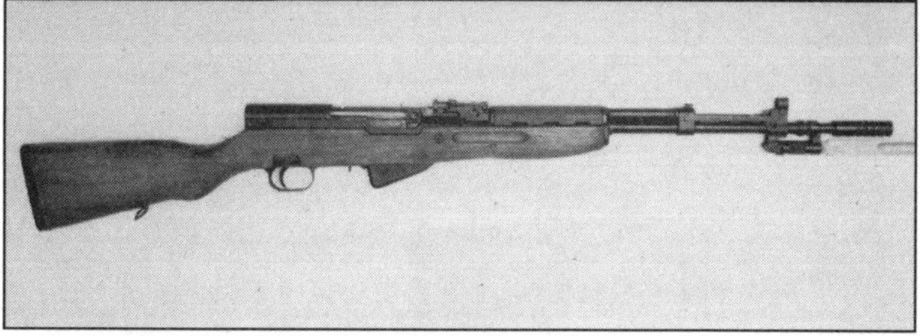

Country of origin: Yugoslavia
Type: self-loading rifle
Used by: Bosnia-Herzegovina; UCK; Yugoslav reservists
Ammunition: 7.62 × 39 mm
Range: 500 m
Feed: 10-round internal box magazine
Weight: 4.1 kg

7.62 mm M70B1/AKM

Country of origin: Yugoslavia
Type: assault rifle
Used by: Bosnia-Herzegovina; Croatia; Slovenia; UCK; Yugoslavia
Ammunition: 7.62 × 39 mm
Range: 400 m
Feed: 30-round detachable curved box magazine
Weight: 3.7 kg (M70b1); 360 g (empty magazine); 870 g (loaded magazine); 210 g (grenade launcher)

7.62 mm SSG 69

Country of origin: Austria
Type: sniper rifle
Used by: UCK; Yugoslav paramilitary forces
Ammunition: 7.62 × 51 mm or 0.243 Winchester
Range: 800 m
Feed: 5-round rotary magazine
Weight: 3.9 kg (empty); 4.6 kg (with telescope)

7.92 mm M76

Country of origin: Yugoslavia
Type: semi-automatic sniper rifle
Used by: Bosnia-Herzegovina; Croatia; Slovenia; UCK; Yugoslavia
Ammunition: 7.92 mm
Range: 1,000 m
Feed: 10-round detachable box magazine
Weight: 4.2 kg
Notes: very similar to the Russian Dragunov sniper rifle.

5.56 mm R4/R5

Country of origin: South Africa
(R5 parentheses)
Type: assault rifle
Used by: Yugoslav special forces
Ammunition: 5.56 × 45 mm
Range: 500 m (400 m)
Feed: 35-round box magazine
Weight: empty, 4.3 kg (3.7 kg); with 35-round magazine, 4.44 kg (3.84 kg)

44 mm RB M57/M80

Country of origin: Germany
Type: anti-tank launcher
Used by: Croatia; Yugoslavia
Calibre/Warhead: 44 mm; projectile, 90 mm/ HEAT
Penetration/Range: 380 mm @ 200 m (effective); 1,300 m (maximum)
Weight: 8.1 kg (launcher); 2.44 kg (projectile)

64 mm RBR-M80

Country of origin: Yugoslavia
Type: light anti-armour weapon
Used by: Yugoslavia
Calibre/Warhead: 64 mm/HEAT
Penetration/Range: 300 mm @ 250 m (effective); 1,280 m (maximum)
Weight: 3 kg (complete); 1.42 kg (launcher); 1.58 kg (rocket)

82 mm M60A

Country of origin: Yugoslavia
Type: recoilless gun
Used by: Croatia; Yugoslavia
Calibre/Warhead: 82 mm/ HEAT M60 projectile range and HEAT M72 with rocket propulsion
Penetration/Range: 250 mm @ 700 m (effective range); 2,000 m (stationary targets)
Weight: 122 kg; round, 7.2 kg

90 mm M79

Country of origin: Yugoslavia
Type: rocket launcher
Used by: Yugoslavia
Calibre/Warhead: 90 mm
Penetration/Range: 400 mm @ 350 m (effective); 1,960 m (maximum)
Weight: 6.2 kg (launcher); 11.2 kg (launcher, loaded); 3.5 kg (rocket)

120 mm RBR M90

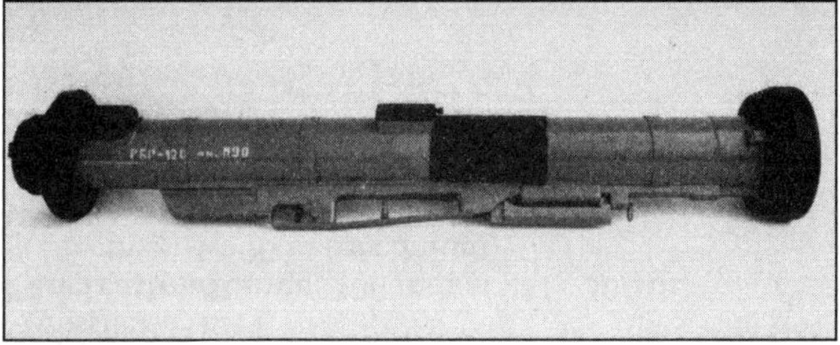

Country of origin: Yugoslavia
Type: rocket launcher
Used by: Croatia; Yugoslavia
Calibre/Warhead: 120 mm/HEAT
Penetration/Range: 800 mm or 2 m reinforced concrete @ 250 m (effective)
Weight: 13 kg (complete); 5.7 kg (launcher); 7.3 kg (rocket); 1.8 kg (explosive charge)

Armbrust

Country of origin: Singapore
Type: short-range anti-armour weapon
Used by: Bosnia-Herzegovina; Croatia; Slovenia; Yugoslavia
Calibre/Warhead: 75 mm (launcher), 67 mm (missile)/ HEAT
Penetration/Range: 300 mm at 0° @ 300 m (effective); 1,500 m (maximum)
Weight: 6.3 kg (weapon); 1 kg (missile)

Maljutka (AT-3 Sagger)

Country of origin: Former Yugoslavia
Type: anti-tank guided missile
Used by: Yugoslavia
Calibre/Warhead: Improved HEAT
Penetration/Range: 520 mm (manual); 600 mm (SACLOS) @ 3,000 m (maximum)
Weight: 11 kg (missile); 7 kg (launch platform); 12.5 kg (guidance unit)

50 mm M-8

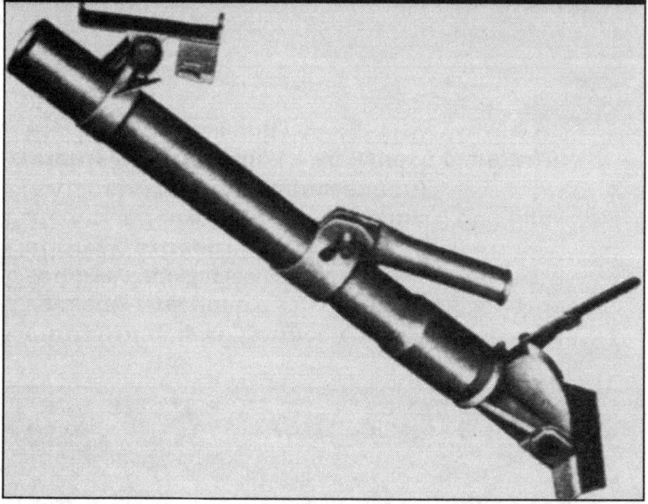

Country of origin: Yugoslavia
Type: platoon mortar
Used by: Bosnia-Herzegovina; Croatia; Macedonia; Slovenia; UCK; Yugoslavia
Calibre/Ammunition: 50 mm/HE bomb weighing about 1 kg; Smoke bomb; Illuminating bomb
Maximum range: 480 m
Weight: 7.3 kg

60 mm M-57

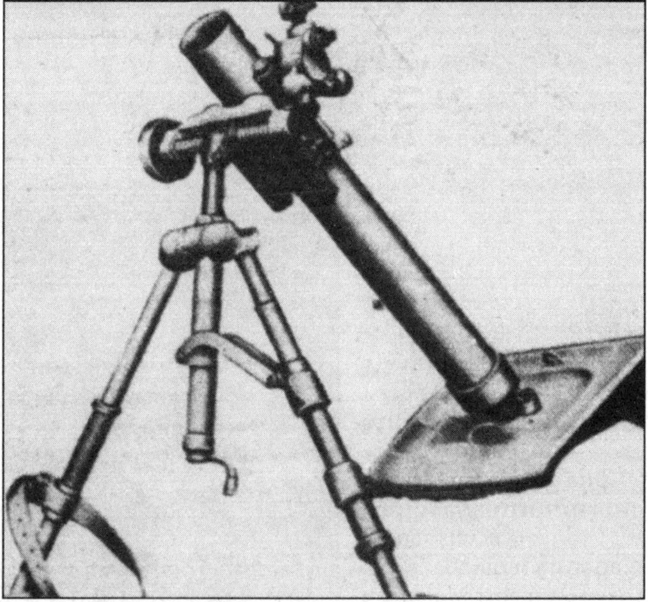

Country of origin: Yugoslavia
Type: company mortar
Used by: UCK; Yugoslavia
Calibre/Ammunition: 60.75 mm/HE; Smoke and Illuminating bombs
Maximum range: 2,540 m
Weight: 5.5 kg (barrel); 4.5 kg (bipod); 8.85 kg (baseplate); 1 kg (sight); 1.35 kg (bomb weight)

60 mm M-70

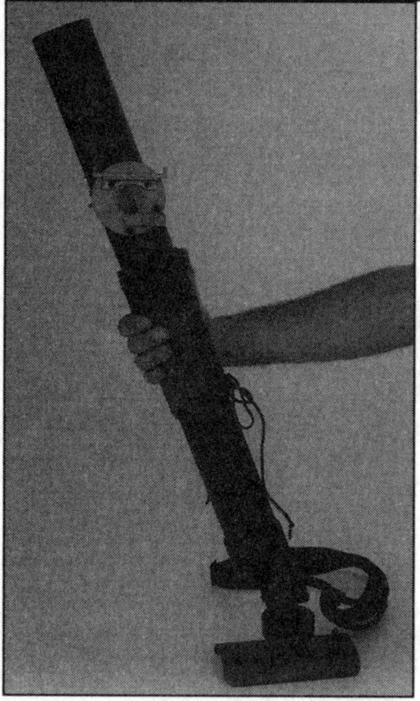

Country of origin: Yugoslavia
Type: lightweight 'Commando' mortar
Used by: Bosnia-Herzegovina; Croatia; Yugoslavia
Calibre/Ammunition: 60.75 mm/M67 and M73 bombs
Maximum range: 2,540 m
Weight: 7.6 kg

60 mm M-90

Country of origin: Yugoslavia
Type: long-range mortar system
Used by: Yugoslavia
Calibre/ Ammunition: 60.75 mm/HE; Smoke and Illuminating bombs; long-range M-90 HE and Smoke WP bombs

Maximum range: 5,208 m
Weight: 32.6 kg (in firing position)

81 mm M-68

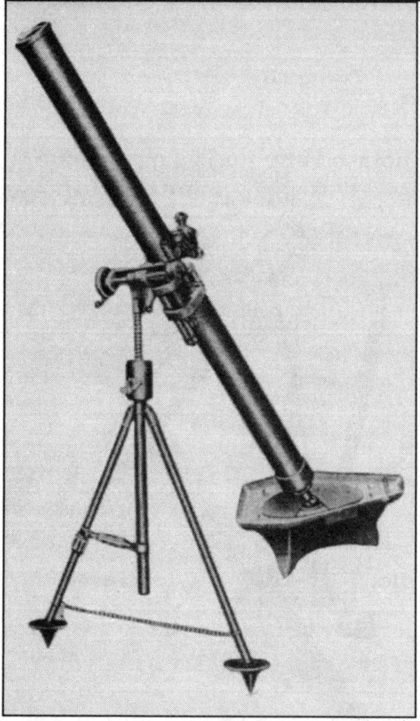

Country of origin: Yugoslavia
Type: battalion mortar
Used by: Bosnia-Herzegovina; Croatia; Yugoslavia
Calibre/ Ammunition: 81 mm
Maximum range: 5,000 m
Weight: 16 kg (barrel); 13 kg (bipod); 11 kg (baseplate); 1.5 kg (sight)

82 mm M-69A

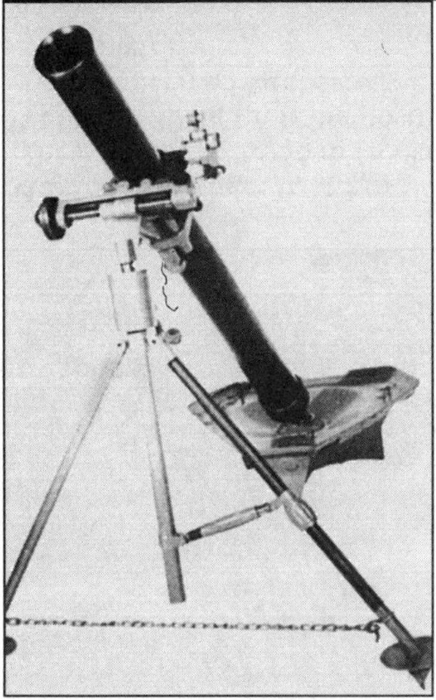

Country of origin: Yugoslavia
Type: battalion mortar
Used by: Croatia; Yugoslavia
Calibre/ Ammunition: 82 mm
Maximum range: 6,050 m
Weight: 45 kg (complete); 14.5 kg (barrel); 14 kg (bipod); 15 kg (baseplate); sight (1.5 kg)

120 mm M-74

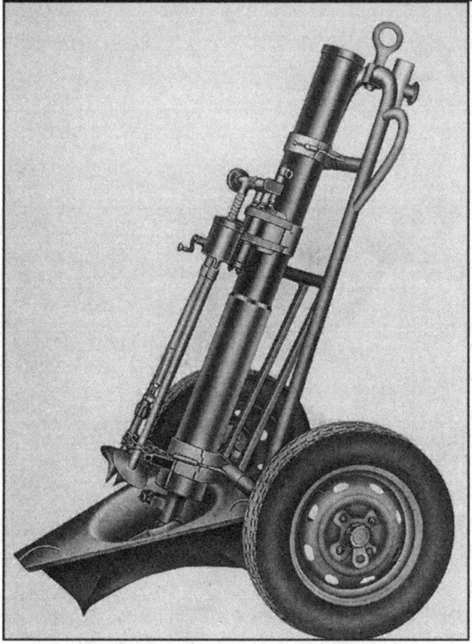

Country of origin: Yugoslavia
Type: heavy mortar
Used by: Bosnia-Herzegovina; Croatia; Yugoslavia
Calibre/ Ammunition: 120 mm/light and heavy HE bombs; a rocket-assisted bomb (fired with or without rocket boost); Smoke, Illuminating and Practice bombs
Maximum range: 6,213 m (light bomb); 5,374 m (heavy bomb); 9,056 m (rocket-assisted bomb)
Weight: 120 kg (in firing position); 208 kg (travelling, with trailer); 45 kg (barrel); 25 kg (bipod); 49 kg (baseplate)

120 mm M-75

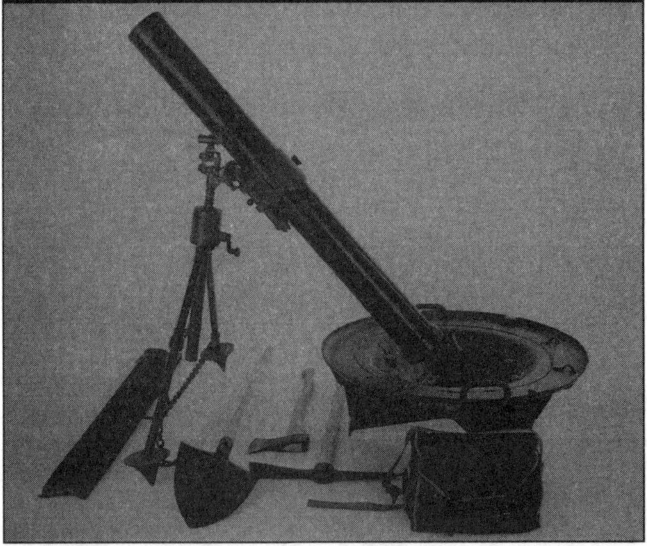

Country of origin: Yugoslavia
Type: light mortar
Used by: Bosnia-Herzegovina; Croatia; Yugoslavia
Calibre/Ammunition: 120 mm/all types of 120 mm ammunition may be fired, as can a rocket-assisted bomb
Maximum range: 6,340 m (light bomb); 5,551 m (heavy bomb); 9,056 m (rocket-assisted bomb)
Weight: 177 kg (in firing position); 263 kg (travelling, with trailer); 65 kg (barrel); 25 kg (bipod); 86 kg (baseplate)

MRUD

Photo: Colin King

Type: AP directional fragmentation
Operation: electrical, tripwire
Metal content: high
Explosive type: plastic
Anti-handling: none
Operating pull: approximately 3 kg
Weight: 1.5 kg
Explosive weight: 900 g
Length: 231 mm **Height:** 89 mm **Width:** 46 mm
Notes: often placed well above ground, can be linked to other mines. In the photograph MRUD is set for electrical initiation.

PMA-1A

Photo: Colin King

Type: AP blast
Operation: pressure
Metal content: very low
Explosive type: TNT
Anti-handling: none
Operating pressure: 3 kg (min)
Weight: 400 g
Explosive weight: 200 g
Length: 140 mm **Height:** 30 mm **Width:** 70 mm
Notes: normally buried a few cm deep and covered completely.

PMA-2

Photo: Colin King

Type: AP blast
Operation: pressure
Metal content: very low
Explosive type: TNT
Anti-handling: none
Operating pressure: 7-15 kg
Weight: 135 g
Explosive weight: 100 g
Diameter: 68 mm
Height: 61 mm
Notes: normally buried with just top of fuze prongs showing. The photograph shows the PMA-2 with safety pin fitted.

PMA-3

Photo: Colin King

Type: AP blast
Operation: pressure
Metal content: very low
Explosive type: tetryl
Anti-handling: none
Operating pressure: 8-20 kg
Weight: 180 g
Explosive weight: 35 g
Diameter: 111 mm
Height: 40 mm
Notes: normally buried a few cm deep and covered completely. The photograph shows the PMA-3 armed without safety band.

PMD-6

Photo: Colin King

Type: AP blast
Operation: pressure
Metal content: high
Explosive type: TNT
Anti-handling: none
Operating pressure: 1-10 kg
Weight: 400 g
Explosive weight: 200 g
Length: 190 mm **Height:** 65 mm **Width:** 90 mm
Notes: possibly of Russian origin or a Chinese copy.

PMN

Photo: Colin King

Type: AP blast
Operation: pressure
Metal content: high
Explosive type: TNT
Anti-handling: none
Operating pressure: 8-25 kg
Weight: 550 g
Explosive weight: 240 g
Diameter: 112 mm
Height: 56 mm
Notes: possibly of Russian origin or a Chinese copy.

PMR-1

Photo: Colin King

Type: AP fragmentation
Operation: tripwire
Metal content: high
Explosive type: TNT
Anti-handling: none
Operating pull: approximately 3 kg
Weight: 2 kg
Explosive weight: 75 g
Diameter: 80 mm
Height (unfuzed): 120 mm
Notes: normally mounted a few cm above the ground on a wooden stake. The photograph shows the PMR-1 with UPM-1 fuze.

PMR-2A

Photo: Colin King

Type: AP fragmentation
Operation: tripwire
Metal content: high
Explosive type: TNT
Anti-handling: none
Operating pull: approximately 3 kg
Weight: 1.7 kg
Explosive weight: 100 g
Diameter: 66 mm
Height (unfuzed): 140 mm
Notes: normally mounted a few cm above the ground on a wooden stake. The photograph show the PMR-2A with UPM-2A fuze.

PMR-3

Photo: Colin King

Type: AP fragmentation
Operation: tripwire
Metal content: high
Explosive type: plastic
Anti-handling: none
Operating pull: 2.7 kg
Weight: 2 kg
Explosive weight: 410 g
Diameter: 77 mm
Height (unfuzed): 128 mm
Notes: can be mounted either way up, above the ground on a metal stake.

PMR-4

Photo: Colin King

Type: AP fragmentation
Operation: tripwire
Metal content: high
Explosive type: TNT
Anti-handling: none
Operating pull: 2-4 kg
Weight: 2 kg
Explosive weight: 200 g
Diameter: 80 mm
Height of mine body: 130 mm
Notes: normally mounted a few cm above the ground on a wooden stake. The photograph shows the PMR-4 with UPM-1 fuze.

POMZ-2 / POMZ-2M

Photo: Colin King

Type: AP fragmentation
Operation: tripwire
Metal content: high
Explosive type: TNT
Anti-handling: none
Operating pull: 1-3 kg
Weight: 2.3 kg
Explosive weight: 75 g
Diameter: 60 mm
Height of mine body: 130 mm
Notes: possibly of Russian origin or a Chinese copy. The photograph shows the POMZ-2 with MUV fuze.

PROM-1

Photo: Colin King

Type: AP bounding fragmentation
Operation: pressure, tripwire
Metal content: high
Explosive type: TNT/RDX
Anti-handling: none
Operating pressure: 9 kg (3 kg pull)
Weight: 3 kg
Explosive weight: 425 g
Diameter: 75 mm
Height: 260 mm
Notes: mine body is normally buried with only fuze visible. The photograph shows the PROM-1 with tripwire fitted.

TM-46

Photo: Colin King

Type: AT blast
Operation: pressure, tilt
Metal content: high
Explosive type: TNT
Anti-handling: possible
Operating pressure: 120-400 kg (21 kg tilt)
Weight: 8.6 kg
Explosive weight: 5.7 kg
Diameter: 305 mm **Height:** 108 mm
Notes: possibly of Russian origin or a Chinese copy.
The photograph shows the TM-46 with tilt rod fuze fitted.

TMA-1

Photo: Colin King

Type: AT blast
Operation: pressure
Metal content: very low
Explosive type: TNT
Anti-handling: possible
Operating pressure: 100 kg
Weight: 6.5 kg
Explosive weight: 5.4 kg
Diameter: 315 mm
Height: 100 mm
Notes: normally buried a few cm deep and covered completely. The photograph shows the TMA-1 with fuze and cap removed.

TMA-2

Photo: Colin King

Type: AT blast
Operation: pressure
Metal content: very low
Explosive type: TNT
Anti-handling: possible
Operating pressure: 100 kg
Weight: 7.5 kg
Explosive weight: 6.5 kg
Length: 260 mm **Height:** 140 mm **Width:** 200 mm
Notes: normally buried a few cm deep and covered completely. The photograph shows the TMA-2 armed.

TMA-3

Photo: Colin King

Type: AT blast
Operation: pressure
Metal content: very low
Explosive type: TNT
Anti-handling: possible
Operating pressure: 180 kg
Weight: 7 kg
Explosive weight: 6.5 kg
Diameter: 265 mm
Height (fuzed): 110 mm
Notes: mine body is often buried with heads of fuzes just above ground. The photograph shows the TMA-3 with one of the three fuzes removed.

TMA-4

Photo: Colin King

Type: AT blast
Operation: pressure
Metal content: very low
Explosive type: TNT
Anti-handling: possible
Operating pressure: 100-200 kg
Weight: 6 kg
Explosive weight: 5.5 kg
Diameter: 284 mm
Height (fuzed): 110 mm
Notes: mine body is often buried with heads of fuzes just above ground. The photograph shows the TMA-4 with all three fuzes fitted.

TMA-5

Photo: Colin King

Type: AT blast
Operation: pressure
Metal content: very low
Explosive type: TNT
Anti-handling: possible
Operating pressure: 100-300 kg
Weight: 6.6 kg
Explosive weight: 5.5 kg
Length: 300 mm **Height:** 110 mm **Width:** 275 mm
Notes: Normally buried a few cm deep and covered completely. The photograph shows the TMA-5 armed.

TMD-1

Photo: Colin King

Type: AT blast
Operation: pressure
Metal content: very low
Explosive type: TNT
Anti-handling: none
Operating pressure: 200 kg
Weight: 7.5 kg
Explosive weight: 5.5 kg
Length: 320 mm **Height:** 140 mm **Width:** 280 mm
Notes: normally buried a few cm deep and covered completely. The photograph shows the training version of the TMD-1.

TMM-1

Photo: Colin King

Type: AT blast
Operation: pressure
Metal content: high
Explosive type: TNT
Anti-handling: possible
Operating pressure: 130-420 kg
Weight: 8.6 kg
Explosive weight: 5.6 kg
Diameter: 300 mm
Height: 90 mm
Notes: normally buried a few cm deep and covered completely. The photograph shows the TMM-1 armed.

TMRP-6

Photo: Colin King

Type: AT shaped charge
Operation: pressure, tilt
Metal content: high
Explosive type: TNT
Anti-handling: possible
Operating pressure: 150-360 kg
Weight: 7.2 kg
Explosive weight: 5.1 kg
Diameter: 290 mm
Height: 132 mm
Notes: can be initiated electrically or by tripwire on tilt rod. Can be used on its side as an off-route mine. The photograph shows the TMRP-6 with safety band fitted.

Special Electronic Fuzes

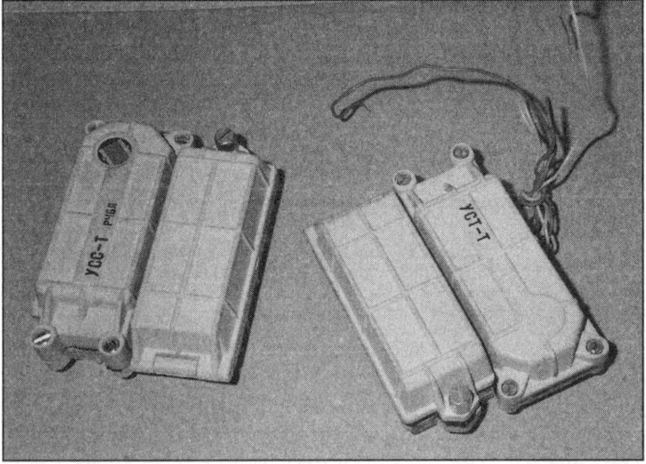

Photo: Colin King

Type: booby trap
Operation: various - see notes
Metal content: medium
Weight: 250 g (incl. battery)
Length: 95 mm **Height:** 37 mm **Width:** 72 mm
Notes: can function by breakwire, sound, tilt, delay, inertia, light, heat, and vibration.

UDOd-1

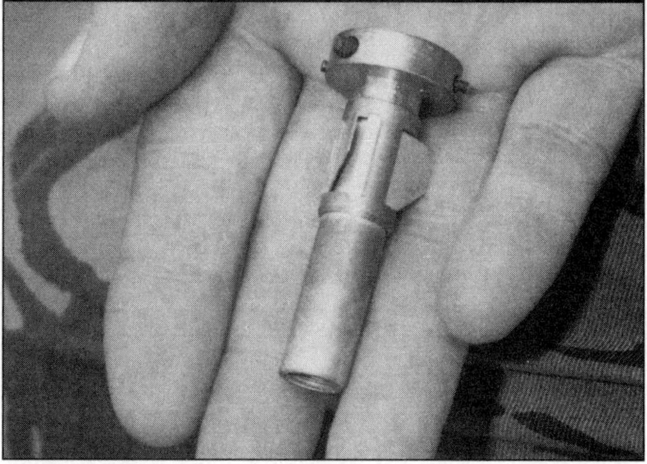

Photo: Colin King

Type: booby trap
Operation: anti-unscrewing
Metal content: high
Length: 55 mm
Cap diameter: 25 mm
Notes: can be used in applications ranging from petrol filler caps to bomb fuze wells.

UDOP-1

Photo: Colin King

Type: booby trap
Operation: pressure release
Metal content: high
Retaining pressure: 3 kg
Length: 80 mm
Notes: the photograph shows the UDOP-1 with safety pin fitted.

UDP-1

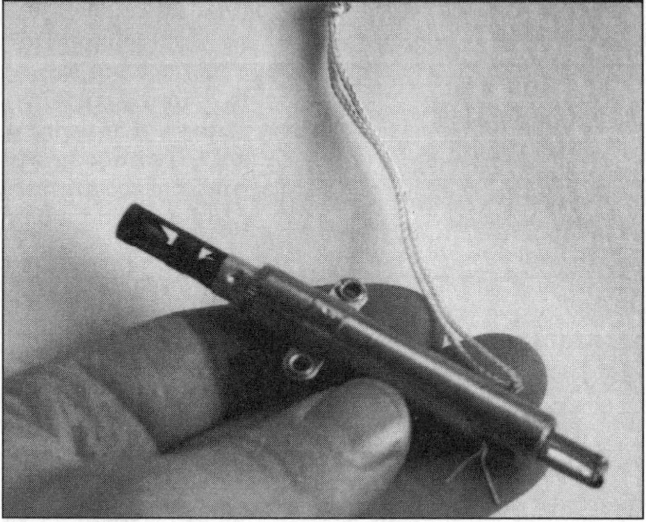

Photo: Colin King

Type: booby trap
Operation: pull
Metal content: high
Operating pull: 3 kg
Length: 70 mm
Diameter: 12 mm
Notes: can be used with mines and demolition blocks. The photograph shows the UDP-1 with safety pin fitted.

UDVK

Photo: Colin King

Type: booby trap
Operation: delay
Metal content: high
Length: 105 mm
Notes: delays ranging from a few minutes to more than a day can be obtained. The photograph shows the UDVK with safety bar fitted.

UDZ-1

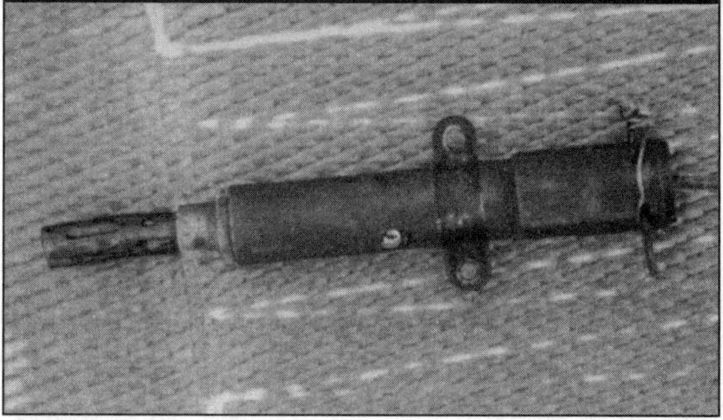

Photo: Colin King

Type: booby trap
Operation: pull, tilt
Metal content: high
Operating pull: 1 kg
Length: 130 mm
Notes: the photograph shows the UDZ-1 with safety clip fitted.

UMNOP-1

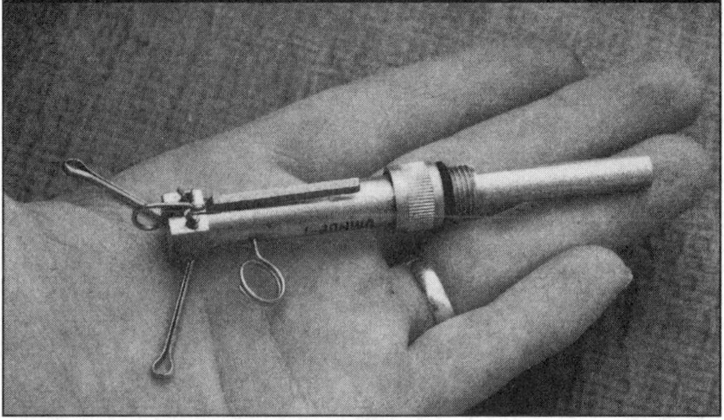

Photo: Colin King

Type: booby trap
Operation: pull, pressure, pressure release
Metal content: high
Operating pull: 1.5-5 kg
Operating pressure: 0.5-5 kg
Retaining pressure: 4 kg
Length: 85 mm
Notes: can be used with mines and demolition blocks.

UMNP-1

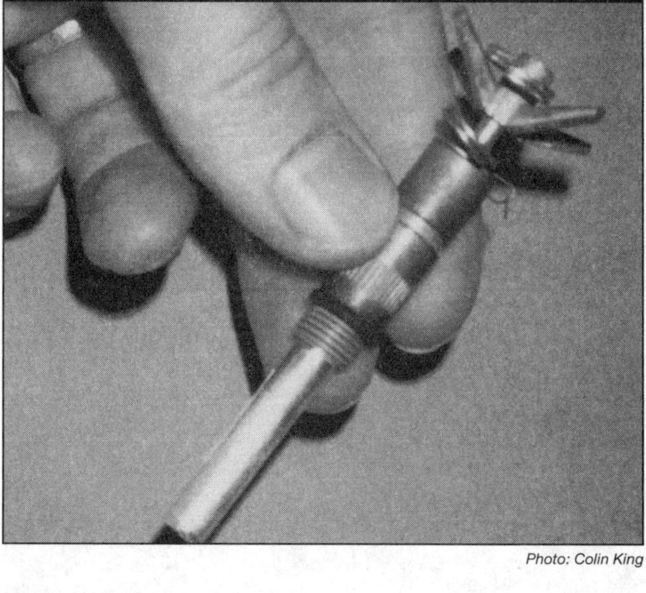

Photo: Colin King

Type: booby trap
Operation: pull, pressure
Metal content: high
Operating pull: 2-7 kg
Operating pressure: 4-7 kg
Length: 81 mm
Notes: can be used with mines and demolition blocks.
The photograph shows the UMNP-1 with safety pin fitted.

UMOP-1

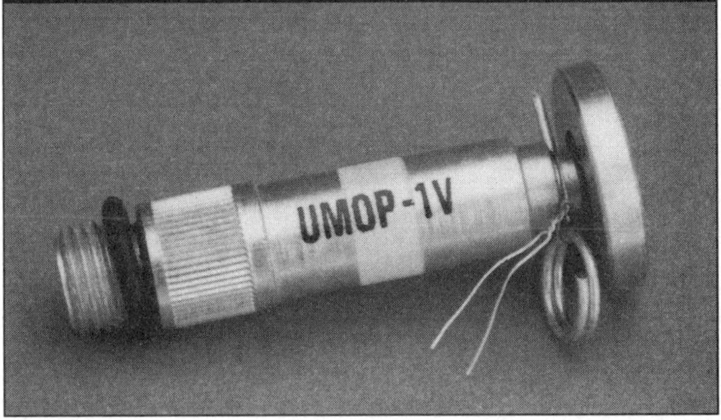

Photo: Colin King

Type: booby trap
Operation: pressure release
Metal content: high
Retaining pressure: 4-15 kg
Length: 76 mm
Notes: can be used with mines and demolition blocks. The photograph shows the UMOP-1 with safety pin fitted.

UMP-1

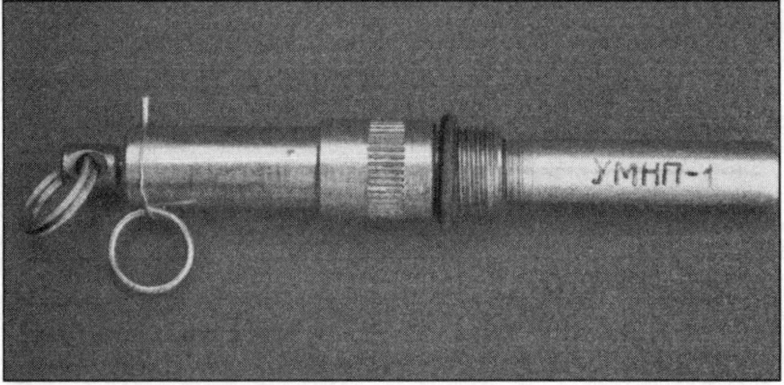

Photo: Colin King

Type: booby trap
Operation: pull
Metal content: high
Operating pull: 1-3 kg
Length: 77 mm
Notes: can be used with mines and demolition blocks. The photograph shows the UMP-1 with safety pin fitted.

UMP-2

Photo: Colin King

Type: booby trap
Operation: pull
Metal content: high
Operating pull: 2-6 kg
Length: 66 mm
Notes: can be used with mines and demolition blocks. The photograph shows the UMP-2 with safety pin fitted.

NOTES

COMMON EQUIPMENT

NOTES

MiG-21 Fishbed

Photo: Michael J. Gething

Country of origin: Russia
Type: interceptor
Used by: Croatia; Hungary; Romania; Yugoslavia
Crew: 1 pilot
Armament: one twin 23 mm cannon; IR or radar guided AAMs; bombs; rockets
Recognition features: mid/small delta wing; swept tail surfaces; nose intake with radar cone
Length: 15.76 m **Wingspan**: 7.15 m

MiG-29 Fulcrum

Country of origin: Russia
Type: interceptor
Used by: Germany; Hungary; Russia; Yugoslavia
Crew: 1 pilot
Armament: one 30 mm cannon; IR or radar guided AAMs; cluster bombs; bombs; rockets
Recognition features: mid/swept wing; twin tails; two ventral intakes; single seat
Length: 17.32 m **Wingspan**: 11.36 m
Notes: the majority of Yugoslavia's single-seat and two-seat MiG-29s were destroyed during NATO airstrikes or shot down trying to intercept NATO fighters. As few as four or five remain operational.

An-26 Curl

Photo: D. Hughes

Country of origin: Ukraine
Type: medium tactical transport
Used by: Bulgaria; Czech Republic; Hungary; Poland; Romania; Russia; Slovakia; Ukraine; Yugoslavia
Crew: 2 pilots; 3 crew
Payload: 5,500 kg or 40 troops
Recognition features: high/tapered wing; two turboprops in long housings; glazed observation bubble
Length: 23.8m **Wingspan**: 29.2 m

Bell 205/412 (Huey)

Country of origin: USA
Type: medium transport helicopter
Used by: Bosnia-Herzegovina; Germany; Greece; Slovenia; Spain; US Marine Corps
Crew: 2 pilots; 2 door gunners
Armament/Payload: 1,760 kg or 14 troops
Recognition features: twin rotors; skids; large side doors; single or twin engines
Length: 12.77 m **Rotorspan**: 14.63 m
Notes: Slovenia operates the four rotor Bell 412 of identical appearance.

Gazelle

Country of origin: France
Type: light observation and attack helicopter
Used by: France; UK; Yugoslavia
Crew: 1 pilot
Armament/Payload: AT-3 anti-tank missiles (Yugoslav aircraft); SA-7 AAMs (French aircraft); HOT anti-tank missiles
Recognition features: Fenestron tail rotor; external engine; glazed bubble cockpit
Length: 11.97 m **Rotorspan**: 10.5 m
Notes: Yugoslav aircraft have a red/white/blue flag on the tailfin; many carry the Red Cross symbol

Ka-25 Hormone

Country of origin: Russia
Type: anti-submarine helicopter
Used by: Russia; Yugoslavia
Crew: 2 pilots
Armament/Payload: depth charges; ASW torpedoes
Recognition features: twin co-axial rotors; quad landing gear; twin tails
Length: 9.75 m **Rotorspan**: 15.74 m

Ka-27 Helix

Country of origin: Russia
Type: anti-submarine helicopter
Used by: Russia; Yugoslavia
Crew: 2 pilots; 1 systems operator
Armament/Payload: 1,000 kg of depth charges; ASW torpedoes
Recognition features: twin co-axial rotors; quad landing gear; twin tails
Length: 11.3 m **Rotorspan**: 15.9 m

MD500

Country of origin: USA
Type: light observation helicopter
Used by: Croatia; US Army
Crew: 2 pilots
Armament/Payload: US Army; TOW; 7.62 mm mini-gun; rockets;
Recognition features: high tail boom; skids; round bubble canopy; round pilot's door window
Length: 7.62 m **Rotorspan**: 8.03 m
Notes: US Army designation AH-6 Little Bird, used to support special forces operations.

Mi-8/Mi-17 Hip

Photo: Richard Strickland

Country of origin: Russia
Type: medium tactical transport helicopter
Used by: Czech Republic; Russia; Yugoslavia
Crew: 2 pilots; 2 crew
Armament/Payload: can carry unguided rockets; 4,000 kg or 30 troops
Recognition features: high tail boom; clamshell rear doors; tricycle landing gear; side-mounted fuel cells
Length: 18.42 m **Rotorspan**: 21.3 m
Notes: the only visible difference between the Mi-8 and Mi-17 is the tail rotor position. The Mi-8 has it on the starboard (right) and Mi-17 on the port (left) side.

Mi-24 Hind

Photo: Paul Jackson

Country of origin: Russia
Type: attack helicopter
Used by: Hungary; Russia; Yugoslavia
Crew: 1 pilot; 1 gunner; 1 door gunner
Armament/Payload: 12.7 mm or 23 mm cannon in nose; AT-3 or AT-2 anti-tank missiles; bombs; rockets; 1,500 kg or eight troops
Recognition features: tandem stepped cockpits; three intakes above pilot; side troop doors; retractable landing gear
Length: 17.51 m **Rotorspan**: 17.3 m

AMX-30

Photo: Antonio Prenda

Country of origin: France
Type: main battle tank
Used by: Bosnia-Herzegovina; Croatia; France; Greece; Spain
Crew: 4
Armament: 105 mm (main); 20 mm cannon or 12.7 mm (coaxial); 7.62 mm (anti-aircraft)
Recognition features: five evenly spaced roadwheels; five-track return rollers
Combat weight: 36,000 kg
Length: 6.59 m **Width:** 3.1 m **Height:** 1.5 m

M60A3

Photo: Antonio Prenda

Country of origin: USA
Type: main battle tank
Used by: Bosnia-Herzegovina; Egypt; Greece; Spain; Turkey
Crew: 4
Armament: 105 mm M68 (main); 7.62 mm (coaxial); 12.7 mm (anti-aircraft)
Recognition features: six small roadwheels; three return rollers; small commander's turret; large round turret
Combat weight: 52,61 kg
Length: 6.94 m **Width:** 3.63 m **Height:** 3.27 m

PT-76

Country of origin: Russia
Type: light amphibious tank
Used by: Croatia; Russia; Yugoslavia
Crew: 3
Armament: 76.2 mm D-56TS
Recognition features: six small roadwheels; vertical hull sides; turret well forward
Combat weight: 14,600 kg
Length: 6.91 m **Width:** 3.14 m **Height**: 2.25 m

T-34

Photo: Paul Beaver

Country of origin: Russia
Type: main battle tank
Used by: Albania; Bosnia-Herzegovina; Croatia; Macedonia; Slovenia; Yugoslavia
Crew: 5
Armament: 85 mm
Recognition features: five large roadwheels; sloped hull sides; high mounted round turret ring
Combat weight: 32,000 kg
Length: 6.19 m **Width:** 2.99 m **Height**: 2.74 m

T-72

Country of origin: Russia
Type: main battle tank
Used by: Bosnia-Herzegovina; Croatia; Czech Republic; Russia; Yugoslavia
Crew: 3
Armament: 125 mm (main); 7.62 mm (coaxial); 12.7 mm (anti-aircraft)
Recognition features: six equally spaced roadwheels; fume extractor - ¾ length of barrel; V-shaped splash plate
Combat weight: 46,500 kg
Length: 6.95 m **Width:** 3.59 m **Height:** 2.28 m

Type 59

Country of origin: China
Type: main battle tank
Used by: Albania
Crew: 4
Armament: 100 mm (main); 7.62 mm (coaxial); 7.62 mm (bow); 12.7 mm (anti-aircraft)
Recognition features: five roadwheels, prominent gap between first and second; no IR searchlight over the barrel; bow machine gun
Combat weight: 36,000 kg
Length: 6.04 m **Width:** 3.27 m **Height**: 2.59 m
Notes: only in service with Albania but very similar in appearance to Yugoslav T-55s.

Type 62

Country of origin: China
Type: light tank
Used by: Albania
Crew: 4
Armament: 85 mm (main); 7.62 mm (coaxial); 7.62 mm (bow); 12.7 mm (anti-aircraft)
Recognition features: five roadwheels, prominent gap between first and second; tapered barrel muzzle
Combat weight: 21,000 kg
Length: 5.55 m **Width:** 2.86 m **Height**: 2.25 m
Notes: a scaled-down version of the Type 59. It was designed to operate in mountainous terrain.

M113

Photo: Antonio Prenda

Country of origin: USA
Type: armoured personnel carrier
Used by: Bosnia-Herzegovina; Belgium; Canada; Germany; Greece, Italy; Spain; US Army
Crew: 2 + 11
Armament: 12.7 mm
Recognition features: five evenly spaced road wheels; box hull; sloped glacis
Combat weight: 11,070 kg
Length: 4.86 m **Width:** 2.68 m **Height**: 1.85 m (to hull top)

MT-LB

Country of origin: Russia
Type: multipurpose tracked vehicle
Used by: Bulgaria; Hungary; Russia; Sweden; Ukraine; Yugoslavia
Crew: 2 + 11
Armament: 7.62 mm
Recognition features: six equally spaced roadwheels; low/wide hull; small turret over commander's position
Combat weight: 11,900 kg
Length: 6.45 m **Width:** 2.86 m **Height**: 1.86 m

YPR-765

Photo: Michael Jerchel

Country of origin: USA
Type: armoured infantry fighting vehicle
Used by: Belgium; Netherlands; Yugoslavia
Crew: 3 + 7
Armament: 25 mm (main); 7.62 mm (coaxial)
Recognition features: five small roadwheels; box hull with sloped rear cut-outs; high square turret
Combat weight: 13,687 kg
Length: 5.25 m **Width:** 2.81 m **Height**: 1.85 m (to hull top, front); 2.007 m (to hull top, rear)
Notes: some captured from Dutch forces at Srebrenica. Believed to be operated by Arkan's Tigers.

BRDM-2

Photo: Jaroslaw Cislak

Country of origin: Russia
Type: armoured reconnaissance vehicle
Used by: Croatia; Macedonia; Russia; Yugoslavia
Crew: 4
Armament: 14.5 mm (main); 7.62 mm (coaxial)
Recognition features: 4 x 4 roadwheels; two raised belly wheels; small round turret or twin ATGW launcher
Combat weight: 7,000 kg
Length: 5.75 m **Width:** 2.35 m **Height**: 2.31 m

BTR-60

Photo: Richard Strickland

Country of origin: Russia
Type: wheeled armoured personnel carrier
Used by: Croatia; Yugoslavia
Crew: 2 + 16
Armament: 14.5 mm (main); 7.62 mm (coaxial)
Recognition features: 8 x 8 roadwheels, troop door above second and third; small round turret above second wheel
Combat weight: 10,300 kg
Length: 7.56 m **Width:** 2.82 m **Height**: 2.05 m
Notes: BTR-60 amd BTR-80 included together in Common section due to striking similarities, note position of troop door.

BTR-80

Country of origin: Russia
Type: wheeled armoured personnel carrier
Used by: Hungary; Russia; Ukraine
Crew: 3 + 7
Armament: 14.5 mm (main); 7.62 mm (coaxial)
Recognition features: 8 x 8 roadwheels, troop door between second and third; small round turret above second wheel
Combat weight: 13,600 kg
Length: 7.65 m **Width:** 2.90 m **Height**: 2.35 m
Notes: believed to be in service with Croatia. Very similar to the BTR-60, note position of troop door.

122 mm 2S1

Country of origin: Russia
Type: self-propelled howitzer
Used by: Russia; Ukraine; Yugoslavia
Crew: 2 + 8
Range: 15,300 km
Recognition features: nine small roadwheels; very low turret at rear; narrow tracks
Combat weight: 15,000 kg
Length: 7.21 m **Width:** 2.85 m **Height:** 2.03 m

105 mm L118

Photo: Antonio Prenda

Country of origin: UK
Type: light gun
Used by: Bosnia-Herzegovina; Spain; UK; US Army
Crew: 5 to 6
Range: 17,200 m
Rate of fire: 3 rds/min (sustained)
Recognition features: tubular trail; recoil dampers diagonal across breech

105 mm M101

Country of origin: USA
Type: howitzer
Used by: Canada; Croatia; Germany; Greece; Slovenia; Turkey; US Marine Corps; Yugoslavia
Crew: 8
Range: 11,270 m
Rate of fire: 10 rds/min (max); 3 rds/min (sustained)
Recognition features: short barrel, no muzzle break; recoil dampers above and below barrel; blast shield
Barrel length: 2.57 m

122 mm D-30J

Country of origin: Yugoslavia
Type: howitzer
Used by: Bosnia-Herzegovina; Croatia; Czech Republic; Russia; Yugoslavia
Crew: 7
Range: 17,300 m
Rate of fire: 6-8 rds/min
Recognition features: large baffles on muzzle break; recoil damper above barrel; towing ring on muzzle break
Barrel length: 4.7 m (with muzzle brake), 4.2 m (without muzzle brake)

12.7 mm NSV

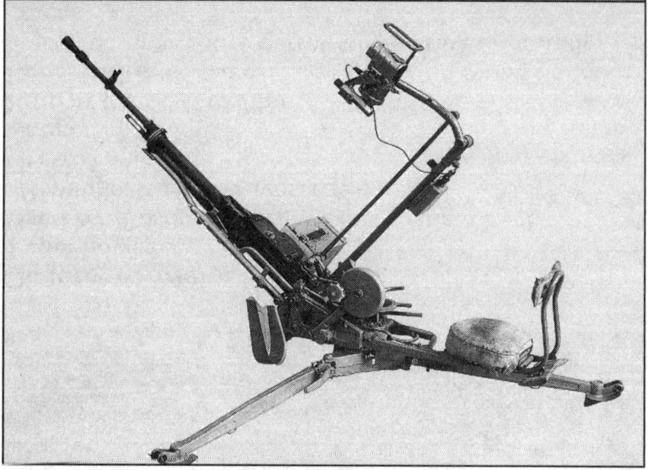

Country of origin: Russia
Type: heavy anti-aircraft machine gun
Used by: Croatia; Russia; Ukraine; Yugoslavia
Crew: 2
Ammunition: normally fires API ammunition with every fourth round being an API-T
Effective range: 1,500-2,000 m
Maximum range: 6,000 m
Recognition features: single barrel; tripod mount can be fitted to AFVs
Weight: 25 kg (without mount)

40 mm Bofors L/70

Country of origin: Sweden
Type: automatic anti-aircraft gun
Used by: Germany; Greece; Italy; Netherlands; Spain; Sweden; Turkey; Yugoslavia
Crew: 4-6
Ammunition: PFHE Mk 2; HCHE; HE-T; APC-T
Effective range: 3,000-4,000 m
Recognition features: single barrel; four-wheeled carriage; shields front and sides
Weight: 2.8 m

SA-7 Grail (Strela-Z/ZM)

Country of origin: Russia
Type: man-portable single-round low-altitude surface-to-air missile system
Used by: Bosnia-Herzegovina; Croatia; Czech Republic; Hungary; Poland; Morocco; Slovenia; Russia; Ukraine; Yugoslavia
Crew (or launcher): 1-2
Maximum effective altitude: 2,000 m (Strela-2); 2,300 m (Strela-2M)
Maximum effective range: 3,200 m (Strela-2); 4,200 m (Strela-2M)
Recognition features: thin body; reloadable grip stock
Weight: 9.2 kg (Strela-2); 9.85 kg (Strela-2M)

SA-14 Gremlin

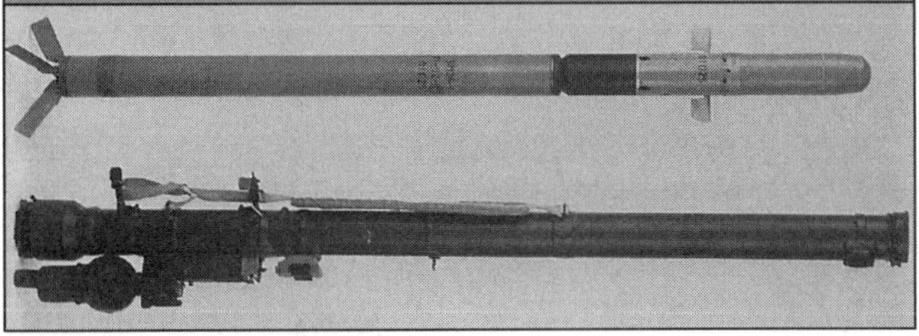

Country of origin: Russia
Type: man-portable single-round low-altitude surface-to-air missile system
Used by: Czech Republic; Finland; Hungary; Poland; Russia; Yugoslavia
Crew (or launcher): single-round disposable with grip-stock and battery/bottle unit
Maximum effective altitude: 1,500 m (approaching target - jets); 3,000 m (approaching target - helicopters and piston-engined aircraft); 1,800 m (receding target - jets)
Maximum effective range: 2,000 m (approaching target - jets); 4,500 m (approaching target - helicopters and piston-engined aircraft); 4,000 m (receding target - jets)
Recognition features: thin body; reloadable grip stock; round bottle at front
Weight: 16 kg (complete weapon system in firing position); 10.3 kg (missile at launch)

MP5

Photo: Paul Beaver

Country of origin: Germany/Iran
Type: sub-machine gun
Used by: Croatia; UCK; UK; US Marine Corps
Ammunition: 9 x 19 mm Parabellum
Range: 150 m (effective)
Feed: 15- or 30-round box magazines
Weight: 2.55 kg
Note: Iranian versions have been delivered to UCK units

7.62 mm Type 56

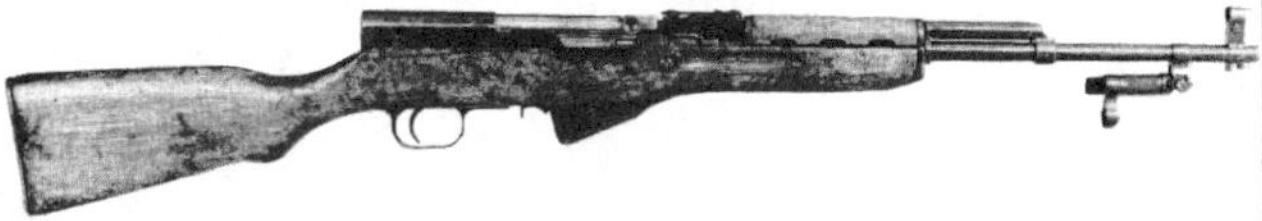

Country of origin: China
Type: semi-automatic rifle
Used by: Albania; UCK
Ammunition: 7.62 × 39 mm (Type 56)
Range: 500 m
Feed: 10-round internal magazine
Weight: 3.85 kg (unloaded)

7.62 mm Type 56C

Country of origin: China
Type: assault rifle
Used by: Albania; UCK
Ammunition: 7.62 × 39 mm (Type 56)
Range: 400 m
Feed: 30-round detachable box magazine
Weight: 3.8 kg

7.62 mm DP/DPM

Country of origin: Russia
Type: light machine gun
Used by: Albania; Croatia; UCK; Yugoslavia
Ammunition: 7.62 mm × 54R
Range: 800 m
Feed: drum, 47 rounds
Weight: 9.1 kg (gun empty)

7.62 mm RP-46

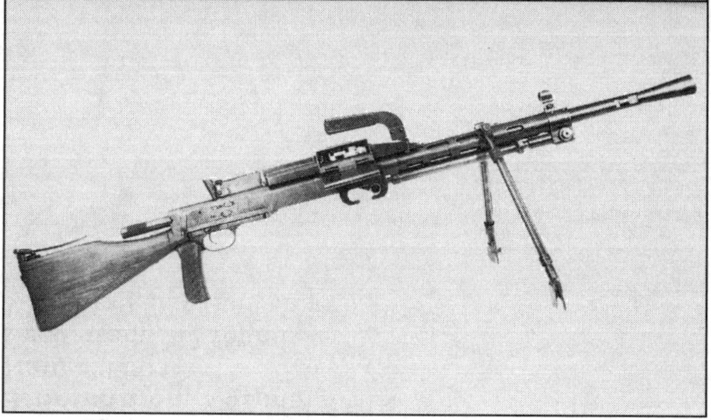

Country of origin: Russia
Type: company machine gun
Used by: Albania; UCK; Yugoslavia
Ammunition: 7.62 × 54R
Range: 800 m
Feed: 250-round belt
Weight: 13 kg (empty)

7.62 mm RPD

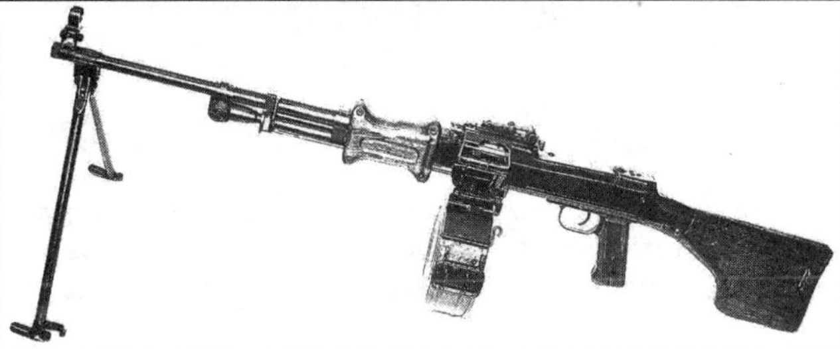

Country of origin: Russia
Type: light machine gun
Used by: Albania; UCK; Yugoslavia
Ammunition: 7.62 × 39 mm M1943
Range: 800 m
Feed: 100-round disintegrating link belt, carried in drum
Weight: 7.1 kg (empty)

7.62 mm M72/RPK

Country of origin: Yugoslavia
Type: light machine gun
Used by: Bosnia-Herzegovina; Croatia; Russia; UCK; Yugoslavia
Ammunition: 7.62 × 39 mm
Range: 800 m (effective), 500 m (anti-aircraft)
Feed: 30-round curved box magazine or 75-round drum
Weight: 5 kg (empty)

7.62 mm M84/PKM

Country of origin: Yugoslavia
Type: general-purpose machine gun
Used by: Bosnia-Herzegovina; Croatia; Russia; UCK; Yugoslavia
Ammunition: 7.62 × 54R
Range: 1,000 m (effective)
Feed: 100- or 250-round belt
Weight: 10 kg

7.92 mm M53/MG34

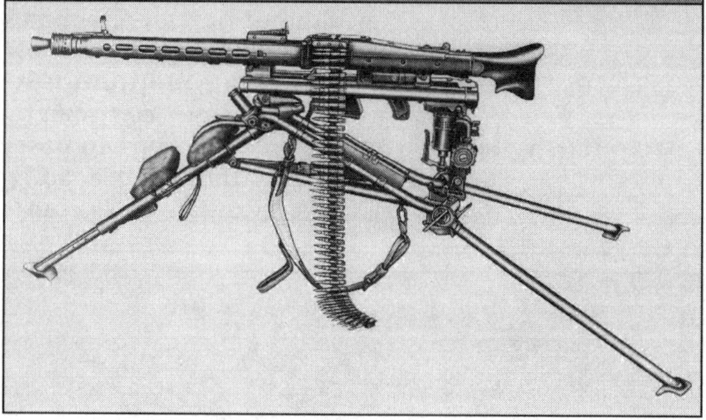

Country of origin: Yugoslavia
Type: general-purpose machine gun
Used by: Bosnia-Herzegovina; Croatia; Germany; Italy (MG34); UCK; Yugoslavia
Ammunition: 7.92 × 57 mm
Range: 500-800 m (bipod effective); 600-1,000 m (tripod)
Feed: 50-round drum magazine or 50-round continuous metal link belt
Weight: 11.5 kg (gun only); 1 kg (bipod); 22 kg (tripod)

0.50 M2HB

Country of origin: USA
Type: standard 0.50 calibre machine gun
Used by: Greece; Italy; UK; US Army; Yugoslavia
Ammunition: 0.50 calibre
Range: 1,000 m
Feed: disintegrating link belt
Weight: 38 kg

12.7 mm DShK-38

Country of origin: Russia
Type: heavy machine gun
Used by: Albania; Yugoslavia
Ammunition: 12.7 × 108 mm
Range: 1,500 m (effective)
Feed: belt
Weight: 35.7 kg (empty)

40 mm RPG-7

Photo: Terry Gander

Country of origin: Russia
Type: portable rocket launcher
Used by: Bosnia-Herzegovina; Croatia; Russia; UCK; Yugoslavia
Calibre/Warhead: launcher, 40 mm
Penetration/Range: 400 mm @ 330 m (max effective, moving targets), 500 m (stationary targets)
Weight: 6.3 kg (launcher with PGO-7 sight)

72 mm RPG-22

Country of origin: Russia
Type: light anti-tank weapon
Used by: Russia; Yugoslavia
Calibre/Warhead: 72.5 mm/HEAT
Penetration/Range: 400 mm @ 250 m (combat)
Weight: 2.7 kg

NATO/COALITION FORCES

NOTES

A-10 Thunderbolt

Photo: Paul Tompkins

Country of origin: USA
Type: close support aircraft
Used by: US Air Force
Crew: 1 pilot
Armament: one 30 mm GAU-8 cannon; Maverick; laser guided bombs; cluster bombs; rockets
Recognition features: low/straight wing; rear podded engines; twin tails
Length: 16.26 m **Wingspan**: 17.53 m
Notes: now painted in all over grey camouflage.

AC-130U Spectre

Country of origin: USA
Type: aerial gunship
Used by: US Air Force
Crew: 2 pilots; 2 flight crew; 7 mission crew
Armament: one 105 mm howitzer; one 40 mm Bofors cannon; one 25 mm or two 20 mm cannons; Hellfire
Recognition features: high/straight wing; four turboprops; guns along port side
Length: 29.79 m **Wingspan**: 40.41 m

AMX

Country of origin: Italy/Brazil
Type: ground attack fighter
Used by: Italy
Crew: 1 pilot
Armament: two 30 mm cannons; Sidewinder; guided and dumb bombs; rockets
Recognition features: high/swept wing; single engine; shoulder intakes
Length: 13.23 m **Wingspan**: 9.97 m

AV-8B Harrier II+

Country of origin: UK/USA
Type: carrier-borne multi-role fighter
Used by: Italy; Spain; US Marine Corps
Crew: 1 pilot
Armament: AMRAAM; Sidewinder; Maverick; 25 mm cannon pod; laser guided bombs; bombs; rockets
Recognition features: high/swept sharp anhedral wing; rounded radar radome
Length: 14.54 m **Wingspan**: 9.25 m

B-1B Lancer

Country of origin: USA
Type: strategic bomber
Used by: US Air Force
Crew: 2 pilots; 2 systems operators
Armament: 34,019 kg of cruise missiles; GPS guided bombs; cluster bombs; mines
Recognition features: mid/swing wing; single tail; ventral engine nacelles
Length: 44.8 m **Wingspan** (spread): 41 m

B-2 Spirit

Country of origin: USA
Type: strategic stealth bomber
Used by: US Air Force
Crew: 2 pilots
Armament: 22,680 kg of cruise missiles; GAM-113 penetration bombs; GPS guided bombs; mines
Recognition features: tailless flying wing; double-W trailing edge; stealth features
Length: 21 m **Wingspan**: 52.4 m

B-52H Stratofortress

Photo: Harry Steele

Country of origin: USA
Type: strategic bomber
Used by: USA
Crew: 2 pilots; 4 systems operators
Armament: 24,750 kg of cruise missiles; Harpoon; bombs; mines
Recognition features: high/swept wing; eight engines; bicycle undercarriage
Length: 49 m **Wingspan**: 56.4 m

EA-6B Prowler

Country of origin: USA
Type: carrier-borne electronic warfare aircraft
Used by: US Navy; US Marine Corps
Crew: 2 pilots; 2 systems operators
Armament: anti-radar missiles
Recognition features: mid/swept wing; fairing on tail fin; prominent fixed refuelling probe
Length: 18.24 m **Wingspan**: 16.15 m

F-5 (MiG-17) Fresco

Country of origin: China/Russia
Type: interceptor
Used by: Albania
Crew: 1 pilot
Armament: one 37 mm cannon; two 23 mm cannons; bombs; rockets
Recognition features: mid/swept wing; nose intake; high mounted tail
Length: 11.26 m **Wingspan**: 9.63 m
Notes: hardly rates as an interceptor the design is almost 50 years old. Albania insists some are still operational.

F-6 (MiG-19) Farmer

Country of origin: China/Russia
Type: interceptor
Used by: Albania
Crew: 1 pilot
Armament: two 30 mm cannons; bombs; rockets
Recognition features: mid/sharply swept wing; nose intake; two engines; low/sharply swept tail surfaces
Length: 14.64 m **Wingspan**: 9.04 m
Notes: the mainstay of the Albanian air force, just over 45 years old.

F-14 Tomcat

Photo: Hachiro Nakai

Country of origin: USA
Type: carrier-borne interceptor
Used by: US Navy
Crew: 1 pilot; 1 systems operator
Armament: one 20 mm cannon; Sidewinder; Phoenix; AMRAAM; GPS guided bombs; laser guided bombs
Recognition features: high/swing wing; twin tails; twin engines
Length: 19.1 m **Wingspan** (spread): 19.54 m

F-15C Eagle

Country of origin: USA
Type: air superiority fighter
Used by: US Air Force
Crew: 1 pilot
Armament: 20 mm cannon; Sidewinder; AMRAAM
Recognition features: high/swept wing; twin tails; single seat
Length: 19.43 m **Wingspan**: 13.05 m

F-15E Strike Eagle

Country of origin: USA
Type: multi-role fighter
Used by: US Air Force
Crew: 1 pilot; 1 systems operator
Armament: 20 mm cannon; Sidewinder; Maverick; anti-radar missiles; laser guided bombs; cluster bombs; rockets
Recognition features: high/swept wing; twin tails; two seats
Length: 19.43 m **Wingspan**: 13.05 m
Notes: very similar to earlier F-15C, the two-seat E model is used primarily as a precision bomber.

F-16 Fighting Falcon

Country of origin: USA
Type: multi-role fighter
Used by: Belgium; Denmark; Greece; Netherlands; Norway; Portugal; Turkey; US Air Force
Crew: 1 pilot
Armament: one 20 mm cannon; Sidewinder; AMRAAM; Maverick; anti-radar missiles; laser guided bombs; cluster bombs; rockets
Recognition features: mid/small delta wing; wing tip missiles; ventral intake
Length: 15.03 m **Wingspan**: 9.45 m

F/A-18 Hornet

Country of origin: USA
Type: carrier-borne multi-role fighter
Used by: Canada; Spain; US Navy; US Marine Corps
Crew: 1 pilot
Armament: 20 mm cannon; Sidewinder; AMRAAM; Maverick; anti-radar missiles; laser guided bombs; cluster bombs; rockets
Recognition features: mid/straight wing; long leading edge extensions; twin tails angled out
Length: 17.07 m **Wingspan**: 11.43 m

F-117A Nighthawk

Country of origin: USA
Type: stealth bomber
Used by: US Air Force
Crew: 1 pilot
Armament: laser guided bombs; GPS guided bombs; anti-radar missiles; Maverick
Recognition features: low/sharply swept wing; butterfly tail; angled body structure
Length: 20.08 m **Wingspan**: 13.2 m

Harrier GR. Mk7

Country of origin: UK/USA
Type: ground attack fighter
Used by: UK
Crew: 1 pilot
Armament: two external 30 mm cannons; Sidewinder; laser guided bombs; cluster bombs; rockets
Recognition features: high/swept wing; sharp anhedral wing; large semi-circular intakes
Length: 14.36 m **Wingspan**: 9.25 m

Jaguar

Country of origin: France/UK
Type: ground attack fighter
Used by: France; UK
Crew: 1 pilot
Armament: two 30 mm cannons; Sidewinder; laser guided bombs; cluster bombs; rockets
Recognition features: high/swept wing; high square intakes; wedge shaped nose
Length: 16.83 m **Wingspan**: 8.69 m

Mirage 2000

Photo: F. Robineau

Country of origin: France
Type: multi-role fighter
Used by: France; Greece
Crew: 1 or 2 pilots
Armament: two 30 mm cannons; Mica and Magic AAMs; laser guided bombs; rockets
Recognition features: tailless delta; small canards; one or two cockpits
Length: 14.36 m **Wingspan**: 9.13 m

Sea Harrier F/A. Mk2

Country of origin: UK
Type: carrier-borne multi-role fighter
Used by: Royal Navy
Crew: 1 pilot
Armament: two external 30 mm cannons; AMRAAM; Sidewinder; anti-radar missiles; bombs; rockets
Recognition features: high/swept wing; sharp anhedral wing; rounded nose cone
Length: 14.17 m **Wingspan**: 7.7 m

Tornado IDS

Country of origin: Germany/Italy/UK
Type: low-level bomber
Used by: Germany; Italy; UK
Crew: 1 pilot; 1 systems operator
Armament: two 27 mm cannons; Sidewinder; anti-radar missiles; laser guided bombs; cluster bombs
Recognition features: high/swing wing; large single tail; large black radar radome
Length: 16.72 m **Wingspan:** 13.91 m (Spread)

C-5 Galaxy

Photo: Harry Steele

Country of origin: USA
Type: heavy-lift transport
Used by: US Air Force
Crew: 2 pilots; 3 crew
Payload: 345 troops or 118,400 kg/two MBTs
Recognition features: high/swept wing; four underwing turbofans; cargo door in nose
Length: 75.54 m **Wingspan**: 67.88 m

C-17 Globemaster

Country of origin: USA
Type: heavy tactical transport
Used by: US Air Force
Crew: 2 pilots; 2 crew
Payload: 200 troops or 76,600 kg/one MBT
Recognition features: high/swept wing; four underwing turbofans; winglets
Length: 53.04 m **Wingspan**: 50.29 m
Notes: can operate from small unprepared airstrips.

C-130 Hercules

Country of origin: USA
Type: medium tactical transport
Used by: Belgium; Canada; Denmark; France; Greece; Italy; Norway; Portugal; Spain; Turkey; UK; US Air Force
Crew: 2 pilots; 3 crew
Payload: 90 troops or 42,000 kg
Recognition features: high/straight wing; four turboprops; large nose radome
Length: 29.79 m **Wingspan**: 40.41 m

C-141 Starlifter

Country of origin: USA
Type: strategic transport
Used by: US Air Force
Crew: 2 pilots; 3 crew
Payload: 150 troops or 90,000 kg
Recognition features: high/swept wing; four turbojets; narrow fuselage
Length: 51.29 m **Wingspan**: 48.74 m

C-160 Transall

Country of origin: France/Germany
Type: medium tactical transport
Used by: France; Germany
Crew: 2 pilots; 1 crew
Payload: 90 troops or 16,000 kg
Recognition features: high/straight wing; two turboprops; long dorsal spine
Length: 32.4 m **Wingspan**: 40 m

G222

Country of origin: Italy
Type: light tactical transport
Used by: Italy
Crew: 2 pilots; 1 crew
Payload: 46 troops or 9,500 kg
Recognition features: high/straight wing; two turboprops; short/wide fuselage
Length: 22.7 m **Wingspan**: 28.7 m

Il-76 Candid

Country of origin: Russia
Type: heavy tactical transport
Used by: Russia; Ukraine
Crew: 2 pilots; 5 crew
Payload: 140 troops or 114,640 kg
Recognition features: high/swept wing; four underwing turbofans; glazed nose
Length: 46.59 m **Wingspan**: 50.5 m

A-109

Country of origin: Italy
Type: light observation and transport helicopter
Used by: Italy; Belgium
Crew: 2 pilots
Armament/Payload: 12.7 mm gun pods; rockets or six troops
Recognition features: tricycle landing gear; ventral fin on boom; pointed nose section
Length: 10.7 m **Rotorspan**: 11 m

A-129 Mangusta

Country of origin: Italy
Type: attack helicopter
Used by: Italy
Crew: 2 pilots
Armament/Payload: Hellfire or TOW anti-tank missiles; Sidewinder; rockets
Recognition features: two stepped cockpits in tandem; fixed landing gear; large dustbin sensor on nose
Length: 12.27 m **Rotorspan**: 11.9 m

AH-1W Cobra

Country of origin: USA
Type: attack helicopter
Used by: Turkey; US Marine Corps
Crew: 1 pilot; 1 gunner
Armament/Payload: one multi-barrel 20 mm cannon; TOW anti-tank missiles; rockets
Recognition features: tandem cockpit; narrow fuselage; skids
Length: 13.87 m **Rotorspan**: 14.63 m

AH-64 Apache

Country of origin: USA
Type: attack helicopter
Used by: Greece; US Army
Crew: 1 pilot; 1 gunner
Armament/Payload: one 30 mm cannon; Hellfire anti-tank missiles; rockets; Stinger air-to-air missiles
Recognition features: tandem cockpit; high tailfin; cannon between main landing gear
Length: 15.54 m **Rotorspan**: 14.63 m

Bo-105

Photo: Richard Strickland

Country of origin: Germany
Type: light attack helicopter
Used by: Germany; Netherlands
Crew: 2 pilots
Armament/Payload: six HOT anti-tank missiles; 1,500 kg or four passengers
Recognition features: skids; bubble canopy; clamshell rear cargo doors
Length: 8.56 m **Rotorspan:** 9.84 m

CH-46 Sea Knight

Country of origin: USA
Type: medium lift transport
Used by: US Marine Corps
Crew: 2 pilots; 2 door gunners
Armament/Payload: two 12.7 mm machine guns; 25 troops or 4,000 kg
Recognition features: tricycle landing gear; twin tandem rotors; rear loading ramp
Length: 13.66 m **Rotorspan**: 15.54 m (each)

CH-47 Chinook

Country of origin: USA
Type: heavy lift transport
Used by: Canada; Greece; Italy; Netherlands; Spain; UK; US Army
Crew: 2 pilots; 2 door gunners
Armament/Payload: two 7.62 mm machine guns; 55 troops or 12,200 kg
Recognition features: four landing wheels; long side pods; twin tandem rotors; rear loading ramp
Length: 15.54 m **Rotorspan**: 18.29 m (each)
Notes: US Special Forces have a number of MH-47E Chinooks to support insertion operations.

CH-53E Super Stallion

Country of origin: USA
Type: heavy lift Marine transport
Used by: US Marine Corps
Crew: 2 pilots; 2 door gunners
Armament/Payload: two or three 7.62 mm machine guns; 55 troops or 13,000 kg
Recognition features: large tailfin with stabiliser; rear loading ramp; long-range fuel tanks on side pods
Length: 22.35 m **Rotorspan**: 24.08 m
Notes: very similar to the earlier Sea Stallion and the US Special Forces MH-53J Pave Low insertion helicopter.

Lynx

Photo: Paul Jackson

Country of origin: UK
Type: light transport/attack helicopter
Used by: UK Army
Crew: 2 pilots; 1 door gunner
Armament/Payload: 7.62 mm machine gun; TOW anti-tank missiles; eight troops or 900 kg
Recognition features: high/narrow tail boom; skids or tricycle landing gear; long nose section
Length: 15.16 m **Rotorspan**: 12.8 m
Notes: Lynx helicopters with the tricycle landing gear cannot operate TOW.

OH-58 Kiowa Warrior

Country of origin: USA
Type: light observation helicopter
Used by: US Army
Crew: 2 pilots
Armament/Payload: Hellfire anti-tank missiles; Stinger air-to-air missiles
Recognition features: large sensor pod above rotors; skids; long/high tail boom
Length: 10.31 m **Rotorspan**: 10.67 m

Puma

Photo: Paul Jackson

Country of origin: France
Type: medium lift transport
Used by: France; UK
Crew: 2 pilots; 1 door gunner
Armament/Payload: 7.62 mm machine gun; 20 troops or 3,200 kg
Recognition features: retractable tricycle landing gear; high tail boom; side pods for landing gear
Length: 14.06 m **Rotorspan**: 15 m
Notes: a stretched version, the Super Puma, is also in service with France.

Sea King Commando

Country of origin: UK
Type: medium lift transport
Used by: UK Royal Navy
Crew: 2 pilots; 1 door gunner
Armament/Payload: 7.62 mm machine gun; 28 troops or 3,800 kg
Recognition features: reverse tricycle landing gear; amphibious hull; single loading door
Length: 17.02 m **Rotorspan**: 18.9 m

UH-60 Blackhawk

Country of origin: USA
Type: tactical transport
Used by: Turkey; US Air Force; US Army
Crew : 2 pilots; 2 door gunners
Armament/Payload: two 7.62 mm or 12.7 mm machine guns; 14 troops or 3,600 kg
Recognition features: high tail fin; reverse tricycle landing gear; some have stub wings with fuel tanks
Length: 15.26 m **Rotorspan:** 16.36 m
Notes: US Special Forces operate covert insertion and armed attack versions.

RQ-5A Hunter

Country of origin: USA/Israel
Type: surveillance and target acquisition UAV
Used by: France; US Army
Payload: TV/FLIR; laser designator; radar and communications jammers
Mission radius: 267 km
Recognition features: twin tail boom; two propellers in tandem; high/straight wing
Length: 6.95 m **Wingspan**: 8.9 m

CL-289

Country of origin: Canada/Germany/France
Type: surveillance UAV
Used by: France; Germany
Payload: aerial reconnaissance cameras; infrared TV system
Mission radius: 200 km
Recognition features: cylindrical fuselage; four tail fins; single turbojet engine
Length: 3.61 m **Wingspan**: 1.32 m

Crecerelle

Country of origin: France
Type: surveillance and target acquisition UAV
Used by: France
Payload: TV/FLIR; synthetic aperture radar or radar and communications jammers
Mission radius: 90 km
Recognition features: tailless delta wing; single pusher propeller; rounded nose cone
Length: 2.74 m **Wingspan**: 3.28 m

Mirach 100 recce

Country of origin: Italy
Type: reconnaissance UAV
Used by: Italy
Payload: TV; infrared and photographic cameras
Mission radius: 250 km
Recognition features: long cylindical fuselage; low/swept wing; four tailfins; one turbojet
Length: 4.13 m **Wingspan**: 1.81 m

Phoenix

Country of origin: UK
Type: surveillance and target acquisition UAV
Used by: UK Army
Payload: thermal imaging camera
Mission radius: 60 km
Recognition features: twin tail boom; single propeller; ventral payload bay
Length: 3.8 m **Wingspan**: 5.5 m

RQ-1A Predator

Country of origin: USA
Type: long-range surveillance and reconnaissance UAV
Used by: US Air Force
Payload: TV; infrared TV; synthetic aperture radar
Mission radius: 3,700 km
Recognition features: long/straight wing; single pusher propeller; three ventral tailfins
Length: 8.13 m **Wingspan**: 14.85 m

Abrams M1A1

Country of origin: USA
Type: main battle tank
Used by: US Army
Crew: 4
Armament: 120 mm (main); 7.62 mm (coaxial); 12.7 mm and 7.62 mm (anti-aircraft)
Recognition features: square slab-sided turret; seven roadwheels; raised engine deck
Combat weight: 57,154 kg
Length: 7.91 m **Width**: 3.65 m **Height**: 2.88 m

Challenger

Photo: Richard Strickland

Country of origin: UK
Type: main battle tank
Used by: UK
Crew: 4
Armament: 120 mm (main); 7.62 mm (coaxial); 7.62 mm (anti-aircraft)
Recognition features: six roadwheels; fabric thermal sleeve; sunken drivers position
Combat weight: 62,000 kg
Length: 8.32 m **Width:** 3.52 m **Height**: 2.95 m

Leclerc

Country of origin: France
Type: main battle tank
Used by: France; UAE
Crew: 3
Armament: 120 mm (main); 12.7 mm (coaxial); 7.62 mm (anti-aircraft)
Recognition features: rounded turret sides; six roadwheels; commander's sight on roof
Combat weight: 54,500 kg
Length: 6.88 m **Width**: 3.71 m **Height**: 2.53 m
Notes: crew reduced to three due to use of automatic loader.

Leopard 1A5

Country of origin: Germany
Type: main battle tank
Used by: Canada; Italy; Greece
Crew: 4
Armament: 105 mm (main); 7.62 mm (coaxial); 7.62 mm (anti-aircraft)
Recognition features: seven equally spaced roadwheels; gun mantle on turret front
Combat weight: 42,400 kg
Length: 7.09 m **Width**: 3.41 m **Height**: 2.76 m

Leopard 2

Photo: Yves Debay

Country of origin: Germany
Type: main battle tank
Used by: Germany; Netherlands
Crew: 4
Armament: 120 mm (main); 7.62 mm (coaxial); 7.62 mm (anti-aircraft)
Recognition features: wedge-shaped turret; seven roadwheels; prominent commander's sight on roof
Combat weight: 59,700 kg
Length: 7.72 m **Width**: 3.74 m **Height**: 3 m

Scimitar

Photo: Richard Strickland

Country of origin: UK
Type: armoured reconnaissance vehicle
Used by: UK
Crew: 3
Armament: 30 mm (main); 7.62 mm (coaxial)
Recognition features: rear mounted turret; five roadwheels; no side skirts
Combat weight: 7,800 kg
Length: 4.79 m **Width**: 2.24 m **Height**: 2.09 m

AMX 10RC

Country of origin: France
Type: wheeled reconnaissance vehicle
Used by: France
Crew: 4
Armament: 105 mm (main); 7.62 mm (coaxial); 7.62 mm (anti-aircraft)
Recognition features: 6 x 6 roadwheels; boat-shaped hull; very long gun barrel
Combat weight: 15,880 kg
Length: 6.35 m **Width**: 2.95 m **Height**: 2.66 m

BRDM-1

Country of origin: Russia
Type: amphibious scout car
Used by: Albania
Crew: 5
Armament: 7.62 mm MG
Recognition features: 4 x 4 roadwheels; boat-shaped hull
Weight: 5,600 kg (unloaded)
Length: 5.7 m **Width:** 2.25 m **Height**: 1.9 m

Centauro

Photo: Richard Strickland

Country of origin: Italy
Type: wheeled reconnaissance vehicle
Used by: Italy
Crew: 4
Armament: 105 mm (main); 7.62 mm (coaxial); 7.62 mm (anti-aircraft)
Recognition features: 8 x 8 roadwheels; very low turret; rear-mounted turret
Combat weight: 25,000 kg
Length: 7.85 m **Width**: 3.05 m **Height**: 2.73 m

Luchs

Photo: C.R. Zwart

Country of origin: Germany
Type: wheeled reconnaissance vehicle
Used by: Germany
Crew: 4
Armament: 20 mm (main); 7.62 mm (anti-aircraft)
Recognition features: 8 x 8 roadwheels in two pairs; small forward turret; crew door in centre
Combat weight: 20,000 kg
Length: 7.74 m **Width**: 2.98 m **Height**: 2.91 m

VBL

Photo: Richard Strickland

Country of origin: France
Type: reconnaissance vehicle; anti-tank vehicle
Used by: France; Greece; Portugal
Crew: 2 or 3
Armament: 7.62 mm; HOT ATGWs
Recognition features: 4 x 4 roadwheels; two separate bulletproof windscreens; gun ring on roof
Combat weight: 3,550 kg
Length: 3.87 m **Width**: 2.02 m **Height**: 2.14 m

AMX-10P

Photo: Pierre Touzin

Country of origin: France
Type: infantry combat vehicle
Used by: France; Greece; UAE
Crew: 3 + 8
Armament: 20 mm (main); 7.62 mm (coaxial)
Recognition features: external main armament; five roadwheels; trim vane on glacis
Combat weight: 14,500 kg
Length: 5.9 m **Width**: 2.83 m **Height**: 2.83 m

BMD-3

Country of origin: Russia
Type: airborne combat vehicle
Used by: Russia
Crew: 3 + 4
Armament: 30 mm (main); 30 mm grenade launcher; 7.62 mm (coaxial); AT-4/5 ATGWs
Recognition features: small, round turret; five small roadwheels; ATGW mounted above turret
Combat weight: 13,200 kg
Length: 6.36 m **Width**: 3.13 m **Height**: 2.55 m

Bradley M2A2

Photo: Steven Zaloga

Country of origin: USA
Type: infantry fighting vehicle
Used by: US Army
Crew: 3 + 6
Armament: 25 mm (main); 7.62 mm (coaxial); twin TOW launcher
Recognition features: six small roadwheels in two pairs; TOW box launcher on turret; side skirts
Combat weight: 22,940 kg
Length: 6.55 m **Width**: 3.61 m **Height**: 2.97 m

Bv206

Country of origin: Sweden
Type: all-terrain armoured personnel carrier
Used by: Sweden; UK
Crew: 4 + 8
Armament: 7.62 mm
Recognition features: twin articulated hulls; two sets of five roadwheels; wide tracks
Combat weight: 7,000 kg
Length: 6.86 m **Width**: 2 m **Height**: 1.9 m

FV 432

Photo: Richard Strickland

Country of origin: UK
Type: armoured personnel carrier; command post; repair vehicle
Used by: UK
Crew: 2 + 10 (maximum)
Armament: 7.62 mm
Recognition features: square body with sloped glacis; five roadwheels; extensive storage on roof
Combat weight: 15,280 kg
Length: 5.25 m **Width**: 2.8 m **Height**: 2.28 m

LVTP-7

Photo: Yves Debay

Country of origin: USA
Type: amphibious assault armoured personnel carrier
Used by: Italy; Spain; US Marine Corps
Crew: 3 + 25
Armament: 12.7 mm (main); some have 40 mm grenade launchers (coaxial)
Recognition features: six roadwheels; boat-shaped bow; small gunner's cupola with machine gun
Combat weight: 23,991 kg
Length: 7.94 m **Weight**: 3.27 m **Height**: 3.26 m

Marder

Country of origin: Germany
Type: infantry fighting vehicle
Used by: Germany
Crew: 3 + 6
Armament: 20 mm (main); 7.62 mm (coaxial)
Recognition features: external main armament; low turret; six roadwheels
Combat weight: 29,207 kg
Length: 6.79 m **Width**: 3.24 m **Height**: 2.98 m

Spartan

Photo: Richard Strickland

Country of origin: UK
Type: armoured personnel carrier; ATGW carrier; Sultan command post; Samaritan ambulance
Used by: UK
Crew: 3 + 4
Armament: 7.62 mm; MILAN on ATGW carrier
Recognition features: five equally spaced roadwheels; no side skirts; large box bodies on Sultan and Samaritan
Combat weight: 8,170 kg
Length: 5.12 m **Width**: 2.24 m **Height**: 2.26 m

Stormer

Country of origin: UK
Type: high velocity missile carrier; reconnaissance vehicle
Used by: UK
Crew: 4
Armament: Starstreak HVM
Recognition features: eight-round missile launcher; six equally spaced roadwheels; long sloping glacis
Combat weight: 12,700 kg
Length: 5.27 m **Width**: 2.4 m **Height**: 2.27 m

VCC-1

Photo: Richard Strickland

Country of origin: Italy
Type: infantry fighting vehicle
Used by: Italy
Crew: 2 + 7
Armament: 12.7 mm (main); 7.62 mm
Recognition features: five equally spaced roadwheels; rear hull slopes inwards; applique armour blocks
Combat weight: 11,600 kg
Length: 5.04 m **Width**: 2.68 m **Height**: 2.55 m
Notes: very similar to the YPR-765

Warrior

Photo: Paul Beaver

Country of origin: UK
Type: infantry fighting vehicle
Used by: UK
Crew: 3 + 7
Armament: 30 mm (main); 7.62 mm (coaxial)
Recognition features: low turret; armour blocks on sides and glacis; six unevenly spread roadwheels
Combat weight: 28,000 kg
Length: 6.34 m **Width**: 3.03 m **Height**: 2.79 m

Bison

Country of origin: Canada
Type: amphibious APC; ambulance; mortar carrier
Used by: Canada
Crew: 3 + 6
Armament: 12.7 mm (main); 7.62 mm (coaxial)
Recognition features: 8 x 8 roadwheels; amphibious hull; square troop compartment
Combat weight: 10,500 kg
Length: 5.96 m **Width**: 2.53 m **Height**: 2.53 m
Notes: the US Marine Corps operates the LAV-25 version with a 25 mm gun turret.

BMR-600

Photo: Pierre Touzin

Country of origin: Spain
Type: armoured personnel carrier; command vehicle; mortar carrier; ambulance
Used by: Spain
Crew: 2 + 10
Armament: 12.7 mm (main)
Recognition features: 6 x 6 roadwheels; amphibious hull; separate wheel arches; external main armament
Combat weight: 14,000 kg
Length: 6.15 m **Width**: 2.5 m **Height**: 2.36 m

Condor

Country of origin: Germany
Type: light armoured personnel carrier
Used by: Malaysia
Crew: 2 + 12
Armament: 20 mm (main); 7.62 mm (coaxial)
Recognition features: 4 x 4 roadwheels; amphibious hull; driver's cab; troop door in hull side
Combat weight: 12,400 kg
Length: 6.47 m **Width**: 2.47 m **Height**: 2.79 m

Cougar/Grizzly

Photo: Richard Strickland

Country of origin: Canada
Type: armoured personnel carrier/fire support vehicle
Used by: Canada
Crew: 3 + 6
Armament: Cougar - 12.7 mm (main); 7.62 mm (coaxial). Grizzly - 76 mm (main); 7.62 mm (coaxial)
Recognition features: 2 + 4 x 4 roadwheels; amphibious hull; shrouded propellers
Combat weight: 10,500 kg (Grizzly)
Length: 5.96 m **Width**: 2.53 m **Height**: 2.53 m

Fuchs

Country of origin: Germany
Type: armoured personnel carrier; reconnaissance vehicle; command post; electronic warfare vehicle
Used by: Germany; UK; US Army
Crew: 2 + 10
Armament: 7.62 mm
Recognition features: 6 x 6 roadwheels; gap between second and third wheels; amphibious hull
Combat weight: 19,000 kg
Length: 6.83 m **Width:** 2.98 m **Height**: 2.3 m

Mamba

Photo: Paul Beaver

Country of origin: South Africa
Type: mine-protected light APC
Used by: UK
Crew: 2 + 9
Armament: none fitted as standard
Recognition features: 4 x 4 roadwheels; large glass windows; high ground clearance
Combat weight: 7,500 kg
Length: 5.53 **Width**: 2.2 m **Height**: 2.59

MAV 5

Country of origin: Italy
Type: light armoured personnel carrier
Used by: Italy
Crew: 2 + 4
Armament: 7.62 mm
Recognition features: 4 x 4 roadwheels; conventional van layout; large windscreen
Combat weight: 4,450 kg
Length: 4.66 m **Width**: 2 m **Height:** 2.15 m

Saxon

Country of origin: UK
Type: armoured personnel carrier; command post; ambulance
Used by: UK
Crew: 2 + 8
Armament: 7.62 mm
Recognition features: 4 x 4 roadwheels; offset driver's cab; commander's cab; high ground clearance
Combat weight: 11,600 kg
Length: 5.17 m **Width**: 2.48 m **Height**: 2.62 m

Type 6614

Photo: Richard Strickland

Country of origin: Italy
Type: light armoured personnel carrier
Used by: Italy
Crew: 1 + 10
Armament: 12.7 mm
Recognition features: 4 x 4 roadwheels; radiator grill above front wheel; side troop door
Combat weight: 8,500 kg
Length: 5.86 m **Width**: 2.5 m **Height**: 2.18 m

VAB

Photo: Richard Strickland

Country of origin: France
Type: armoured personnel carrier; infantry fighting vehicle; anti-tank vehicle; command post; mortar carrier
Used by: France; UAE
Crew: 2 + 10
Armament: 20 mm or 12.7 mm (main); 7.62 mm (coaxial)
Recognition features: 4 x 4 roadwheels; numerous windows; external main armament
Combat weight: 13,000 kg
Length: 5.98 m **Width**: 2.49 m **Height**: 2.06 m

XA-180

Country of origin: Finland
Type: armoured personnel carrier; ambulance
Used by: Baltic Battalion; Finland; Netherlands; Norway; Sweden
Crew: 2 + 10
Armament: 12.7 mm
Recognition features: 6 x 6 roadwheels; driver's cab forward of front wheels; small turret to rear
Combat weight: 15,500 kg
Length: 7.35 m **Width**: 2.9 m **Height**: 2.6 m

120 mm 2S9 Anona

Photo: Richard Strickland

Country of origin: Russia
Type: airborne artillery system
Used by: Russia
Crew: 4
Range: 13,000 m
Recognition features: high glacis plate; six small roadwheels; very narrow tracks
Combat weight: 8,700 kg
Length: 6.02 m **Width**: 2.63 m **Height**: 2.3 m

155 mm AS90

Country of origin: UK
Type: self-propelled howitzer; recovery vehicle
Used by: UK
Crew: 5
Armament: 155 mm howitzer (main); 12.7 mm or 7.62 mm (anti-aircraft)
Range: 40,000 m (maximum)
Recognition features: long/low hull; stowage boxes on turret; square barrel mount
Combat weight: 45,000 kg
Length: 7.2 m **Width**: 3.4 m **Height**: 3 m

155 mm AUF-1

Photo: Pierre Touzin

Country of origin: France
Type: self-propelled howitzer
Used by: France
Crew: 4
Armament: 155 mm howitzer (main); 7.62 mm (anti-aircraft)
Range: 29,000 m (maximum)
Recognition features: AMX-30 hull; wendy house turret; no rear hull access
Combat weight: 42,000 kg
Length: 6.7 m **Width**: 3.15 m **Height**: 3.25 m

155 mm M109 Paladin

Photo: Richard Strickland

Country of origin: USA
Type: self-propelled howitzer; armoured resupply vehicle
Used by: Belgium; Canada; Germany; Greece; Italy; Netherlands; Spain; US Army
Crew: 6
Armament: 155 mm howitzer (main); 12.7 mm (anti-aircraft)
Range: 18,000 m
Recognition features: seven small roadwheels; flat hull sides; large muzzle break
Combat weight: 24,948 kg
Length: 6.19 m **Width**: 3.15 m **Height**: 3.28 m

120 mm 120RT

Country of origin: France
Type: heavy mortar
Used by: Belgium; Canada; France; Germany; Italy; Netherlands
Crew: 4
Range: 13,000 m
Rate of fire: 18 rnds/min
Recognition features: short barrel; twin-wheeled carriage; small stool needed to load bomb
Barrel length: 2.06 m

MLRS

Country of origin: USA
Type: multiple rocket launch system
Used by: France; Germany; Greece; Italy; Netherlands; Turkey; UK; US Army
Crew: 3
Salvo: 12 x 227 mm rockets
Range: 31,000 m
Recognition features: trainable box rocket launcher; cab with slatted shutters; six roadwheels in three pairs
Combat weight: 25,191 kg
Length: 6.97 m **Width**: 2.97 m **Height**: 2.62 m

Glossary

AA: Anti-Aircraft
AAA: Anti-Aircraft Artillery
AAM: Air-to-Air Missile
ABiH: *Armija Bosna I Herzegovina* (Army of Bosnia-Herzegovina)
AC: Alternating Current
ACEATM: Aimed Controlled Effect Anti-Tank Mine
ACEM: Aimed Controlled Effect Mine
ACP: Airfield Clearance Plough
ACRV: Armoured Command and Reconnaissance Vehicle
ACS: Advanced Countermine System
ACV: Armoured Combat Vehicle
ADAM: Area Denial Artillery Munition
ADATS: Air Defence Anti-Tank System
ADP: Accelerated Demining Programme
ADSM: Artillery Delivered Scatterable Mine
AEW: Airborne Early Warning
AFCS: Automatic Fire Control Systems
AFSV: Armoured Fire Support Vehicle
AGM: Air-to-Ground Missile
AGV: Assault Gun Vehicle
AFV: Armoured Fighting Vehicle
AIFV: Armoured Infantry Fighting Vehicle
AIM: Air Intercept Missile
AHD: Anti-Handling Device
AHM: Anti-Helicopter Mine
ALARM: Air-Launched Anti-Radiation Missile
ALCM: Air-Launched Cruise Missile
AMDS: Anti-Missile Discarding Sabot
AMIDS: Airborne Minefield Detection System

AMMAD: Anti-Magnetic Mine Actuation Device
AMRAAM: Advanced Medium Range Air-to-Air Missile
AMS: Advanced Mortar System
AMS-H: Advanced Missile System - Heavy
Anhedral: downward slope of wing from root to tip
AP: Armour-Piercing
APC: Armoured Personnel Carrier
APDS: Armour-Piercing Discarding Sabot
APFIDS: Armour-Piercing Fragmentation Incendiary Discarding Sabot
APFSDS: Armour-Piercing Fin-Stabilised Discarding Sabot
APGM: Autonomous Precision-Guided Munition
APHE: Armour-Piercing High Explosive
API: Armour-Piercing Incendiary
APM: Anti-Personnel Mine
APS: Artillery Pointing System
APSE: Armour-Piercing Secondary Effect
APT: Armour-Piercing Tracer
APV: Armoured Patrol Vehicle
ARV: Armoured Recovery Vehicle
ASM: Air-to-Surface Missile
ASRAAM: Advanced Short-Range Air-to-Air Missile
ASTAMIDS: Airborne Standoff Minefield Detection System
ASTOVL: Advanced Short Take-Off and Vertical Landing
ASV: Ammunition Supply Vehicle
AT: Anti-Tank
ATDS: Airborne Tactical Data System
ATG: Anti-Tank Gun
ATGW: Anti-Tank Guided Weapon
ATM: Anti-Tank Mine
ATMDS: Anti-Tank Mine Dispensing System
AWACS: Airborne Warning and Control System

BAI: Battlefield Air Interdiction
BAC: Battle Area Clearance
BLU: Bomb Live Unit
BT: Booby Trap
BVR: Beyond Visual Range

C^3: Command, Control and Communications
C^3I: Command, Control, Communications and Intelligence
CBU: Cluster Bomb Unit
CBU: Cost of Bomb Unit
CDS: Central Disposal Site
CEP: Circular Error Probability (50/50 chance of being hit inside or outside in bombing, missile attack or gunnery)
CLAMS: Clear Lane Marking System
CLEWP: Clear Lane Explosive Widening Path
CMT: Counter-Mine Training
CMV: Combat Mobility Vehicle
COIN: Counter Insurgency
CP: Command Post
CPV: Command Post Vehicle
CWS: Common Weapon Sight

DC: Direct Current
DINS: Digital Inertial Navigation System
DOD: US Department of Defense

ECCM: Electronic Counter-Countermeasures
ECM: Electronic Countermeasures
EFP: Explosively Formed Projectile/Penetrator
ELF: Extreme Low Frequency
ELINT: Electronic Intelligence
EMP: Engineering Mine Plough
EOD: Explosive Ordnance Disposal

ERA: Explosive Reactive Armour
ERFB: Extended Range Full-Bore
ERFB-BB: Extended Range Full-Bore-Base Bleed
ESM: Electronic Support Measures
EW: Electronic Warfare

FAE: Fuel Air Explosive
FARS: Field Artillery Rocket System
FASCAM: Family of Scatterable Mines
FCS: Fire-Control System
Fenestron: helicopter tail rotor that looks like a fan
FFE: Free From Explosive
FG: Field Gun
FH: Field Howitzer
FIBUA: Fighting In Built-Up Areas
FLIR: Forward-Looking Infra-Red
FOV: Field Of View
FRAG: Fragmentation
FROG: Free Rocket Over Ground
FWAM: Full-Width Attack Mine
FWMP: Full-Width Mine Plough

GBU: Glide Bomb Unit
GEMSS: Ground Emplaced Mine-Scattering System
GH: Gun-Howitzer
GPMG: General-Purpose Machine Gun
GPR: Ground Penetrating Radar
GPS: Global Positioning System
GPS: Gunner's Primary Sight

HARM: High Speed Anti-Radiation Missile
HCHE: High-Capacity High Explosive
HE: High Explosive

HE-APERS: High-Explosive Anti-Personnel
HEAP-T: High-Explosive Anti-Personnel - Tracer
HEAT: High-Explosive Anti-Tank
HEAT-FS: High-Explosive Anti-Tank-Fin-Stabilised
HEAT-MP: High-Explosive Anti-Tank-Multi Purpose
HEAT-MP(P): High-Explosive Anti-Tank-Multi Purpose (Practice)
HEAT-T: High-Explosive Anti-Tank - Tracer
HEAT-T-HVY: High-Explosive Anti-Tank - Tracer - Heavy
HEAT-T-MP: High-Explosive Anti-Tank - Tracer - Multipurpose
HEAT-TP-T: High-Explosive Anti-Tank-Target Practice-Tracer
HEDP: High-Explosive Dual-Purpose
HE-FRAG: High-Explosive Fragmentation
HE-FRAG-FS: High-Explosive Fragmentation-Fin-Stabilised
HE-FS: High-Explosive-Fin-Stabilised
HEI: High-Explosive Incendiary
HEIT: High-Explosive Incendiary Tracer
HERA: High-Explosive Rocket-Assisted
HE-S: High-Explosive-Spotting
HESH: High-Explosive Squash Head
HESH-T: High-Explosive Squash Head-Tracer
HE-T: High-Explosive Tracer
HET-PF: High-Explosive Tracer-Percussion Fuze
HET-SD: High-Explosive Tracer-Self-Destruct
HMG: Heavy Machine Gun
HMLC: High-Mobility Load Carrier
HMMWV: High-Mobility Multi-Purpose Wheeled Vehicle
HOT: *Haut subsonique Optiquement Teleguide tire d'un tube* (French anti-tank missile)
HV: *Hrvatska Vojska* (Croatian Army)

HVAP: High Velocity Armour Piercing
HVAR: High-Velocity Aircraft Rocket
HVO: *Hrvatska Vojska Obrane* (Croatian Defence Council)

IDS: Interdictor/Strike
IED: Improvised Explosive Device
IFF: Identification Friend or Foe
IFOR: Implementation Force
IFV: Infantry Fighting Vehicle
IMF: Improved Mine Fuze
IOE: Irregular Outer Edge
IR: Infra-Red
ISU: Integrated Sight Unit

JSTARS: Joint Surveillance and Target Attack Radar System (US Army/Navy)
JTIDS: Joint Tactical Information Distribution System

KFOR: Kosovo Force
KLA: Kosovo Liberation Army (also see UCK)

LAAG: Light Anti-Aircraft Gun
LANTIRN: Low Altitude Navigation and Targeting Infra-Red for Night
LAV: Light Assault Vehicle (US)
LAV-AD: Light Armoured Vehicle - Air Defense
LAW: Light Anti-Tank Weapon
LED: Light Emitting Diode
LLAD: Low-Level Air Defence
LMG: Light Machine Gun
LMP: Land-Mine Protocol
LMW: Land-Mine Warfare
LOSAT: Line Of Sight Anti-Tank

MAC: Mine Action Centre
MACS: Magnetic Countermine System
MAPED: Mine Anti-Personnel Effect Directional
MAT: Mine Awareness Training
MBT: Main Battle Tank
MCAP: Mine-Clearing/Armour Protection
MCBS: Mine-Clearing Blade System
MCLOS: Manual Command to Line-of-Sight
MCM: Mine Countermeasures
MCP: Mine Clearance Programme
MCRV: Mechanised Combat Repair Vehicle
MCV: Mechanised Combat Vehicle
MDV: Mine Detection Vehicle
MFC: Mortar Fire Controller
MG: Machine Gun
MICLIC: Mine-Clearing Line Charge
MICV: Mechanised Infantry Combat Vehicle
MIDAP: Minefield Detection Algorithm and Processor
MILAN: *Missile d'Infantrie Leger Anti-char* (light infantry anti-tank missile)
MIRADOR: Minefield Reconnaissance and Detector System
MLRS: Multiple Launch Rocket System
MOPMS: Modular Pack Mine System
MOUT: Military Operations in Urban Terrain
MPV: Multi-Purpose Vehicle
MRAV: Multi-Role Armoured Vehicle
MRL: Multiple Rocket Launcher
MRS: Multiple Rocket System
MSTAR: Man-Portable Surveillance and Target Acquisition Radar
MTI: Moving Target Indication
MUP: *Ministarstvo Unutrasnjih Poslova* (Serbian Interior Ministry Police)

NATO: North Atlantic Treaty Organisation
NBC: Nuclear, Biological, and Chemical
NGO: Non-Governmental Organisation
NOE: Nap Of-the-Earth (low-flying in military aircraft, using natural cover of hills, trees etc)
NVG: Night Vision Goggles
NVS: Night Vision System

OEW: Ordnance and Explosive Waste
OOTW: Operations Other Than War
ORATMS: Off-Route Anti-Tank Mine System
OSCE: Organisation for Security and Co-operation in Europe (formerly the CSCE)
OTH: Over The Horizon
OTHT: Over The Horizon Targeting
OZ: Operational Zones (UCK)

PE: Plastic Explosive
PETN: Pentaerythritetranitrate (high explosive)
PFD: Proximity Fuze Disconnector
PFHE: Pre-Fragmented High Explosive
PFPX: Pre-Fragmented Proximity Fuzed
PGM: Precision Guided Munition
Port: the left side, looking forward

RAAMS: Remote Anti-Armour Mine System
RAMBS: Rapid Anti-Personnel Minefield Breaching System
RAP: Rocket-Assisted Projectile
RAPI: Reactive Armour Protection
RDM: Remotely Delivered Mine
RHA: Rolled Homogeneous Armour
RMID: Road Mine Detector
RMG: Ranging Machine Gun

ROMANS: Rapid Operational Minefield Attack and Neutralisation System
ROR: Range Only Radar
RP: Rocket-Propelled
RPG: Rocket-Propelled Grenade
RPV: Remotely Piloted Vehicle
RR: Recoilless Rifle

SACLOS: Semi-Automatic Command to Line-Of-Sight
SADARM: Sense And Destroy Armor (US)
SAM: Surface-to-Air Missile
SAR: Search And Rescue
SDB: *Sluzba Drzavne Bezbednost* (Yugoslav state security service)
SEAD: Suppression of Enemy Air Defences
SFOR: Stabilisation Force
SIGINT: Signals Intelligence
ShP: *Shtabi i Përgjithshëm* (the UCK General Staff)
SLAM: Stand-Off Land Attack Missile
SLAR: Side-Looking Airborne Radar
SLUFAE: Surface-Launched Unit, Fuel-Air Explosive
SM: Scatterable Mine
SMCD: Scatterable Mine-Clearing Device
SMG: Sub-Machine Gun
SMP: Surface Mine Plough
SMS: Scatterable Mine System
SP: Self-Propelled
SPAAG: Self-Propelled Anti-Aircraft Gun
SPAAM: Self-Propelled Anti-Aircraft Missile
SPAG: Self-Propelled Assault Gun
SPATG: Self-Propelled Anti-Tank Gun
SPG: Self-Propelled Gun
SPH: Self-Propelled Howitzer

SPL: Self-Propelled Launcher
SPM: Self-Propelled Mortar
SRAAM: Short Range Air-to-Air Missile
SRAM: Short Range Attack Missile
SSM: Surface-to-Surface Missile
Starboard: the right side, looking forward
STOL: Short Take-Off and Landing
STORM: Sensored Tactical Off-Road Mine
STOVL: Short Take-Off and Vertical Landing
SUMMADE: System Universal Modular Mine And Demolition Explosives

TACMS: Tactical Missile System (US)
TCU: Tactical Control Unit
TD: Tank Destroyer
TEL: Transporter-Erector-Launcher
TI: Thermal Imaging
T/MDV: Towed/Mine Detection Vehicle
TNT: Trinitrotoluene (high explosive)
TOW: Tube-launched Optically-tracked Wire-guided (anti-tank missile)
TPFSDS-T: Target Practice Fin-Stabilised Discarding Sabot - Tracer
TWMP: Track Width Mine Plough

UAV: Unmanned Aerial Vehicle
UCK: *Ushtria Çlirimtare e Kosovës* (Kosovo Liberation Army)
UHF: Ultra-High Frequency
UMIDS: Universal Mine-Dispensing System
UNHCR: United Nations High Commission for Refugees
UNPROFOR: United Nations Protection Force
USAF: United States Air Force

USMC: United States Marine Corps
USN: United States Navy
UXO: Unexploded Ordnance

VJ: *Vojska Jugoslavije* (Yugoslav Army)
VHF: Very High Frequency
VLSMS: Vehicle-Launched Scatterable Mine System
VMRMDS: Vehicle-Mounted Road Mine Detector System
VOD: Velocity Of Detonation
VRS: *Vojska Republika Srpska* (Bosnian Serb Army)
VSTOL: Vertical/Short Take-Off and Landing

WAAPM: Wide Area Anti-Personnel Mine
WAM: Wide Area Mine
WASPM: Wide Area Side-Penetrating Mine

Index

A

B

Editors
David Rendall
Mark Stenhouse

Publisher: Geopolitical
John Boatman

Managing Editor
Mike Bryant

Specialist Advisors
Paul Beaver (Aviation and on the ground reporting)
Peter Felstead (Jane's Intelligence Review)
Christopher F Foss (Armour and Artillery)
Terry Gander (Infantry Weapons)
Colin King (Mine Warfare)
Kenneth Munson (Unmanned Aerial Vehicles)

Major Photographic Contributors
Yves Debay
Paul Jackson
Antonio Prlenda
Richard Strickland
David Taylor at SFOR Informer

Production/Design Team
Kevan Box (Electronic Photographs)
Harriet Harding (Photographs and Rank Structure)
Christine Lawrence (Cover Design and Maps)
Jane Lawrence (Production and Administration Management)
Lynette Murphy (Page Layout)
Katie Rendall (Original Rank Artwork)
Anita Slade (Page Layout and Overall Design)

Editorial
Joanne Fenwick
Rebecca Irons
Chris Jessup
Steve Martin